The Integrity Vow

ENGAGING YOUR AUTHENTIC SELF

Ryan Hodge

ISBN-13: 9781976239526
ISBN-10: 1976239524

Dedication

For My Beautiful Sons: Tyler, Nathan and Justin

"May the wind always be at your back and the
sun upon your face, and the winds of destiny
carry you aloft to dance with the stars."

-GEORGE JUNG

Table of Contents

Introduction

"The soul is dyed the color of its thoughts. Think only
on those things that are in line with your principles and
can bear the light of day. The content of your character
is your choice. Day by day, what you choose, what you
think and what you do is who you become. Your integrity
is your destiny...it is the light that guides your way."

-HERACLITUS

I WAS ON A PLANE, flying to visit a friend, and I didn't feel well. I was
dizzy, nauseous and experiencing anxiety, as if the plane were going
to crash. In essence, my life was seemingly crashing all around me
and I couldn't stand the thought of living anymore or the feelings
that I was enduring. I was tired of feeling sick, both mentally and
physically, to the point of exhaustion. I wasn't sleeping properly or
eating right. There were days I would not eat at all, but I would fuel
up on bottles of red wine at night and wake up in a sweat feeling as
though I did not know where I was. To say that I was unaligned and
out of integrity would be an understatement.

This was not good as I had a lot going on in my life. I was married with three wonderful children and had a thriving real estate
business.

My real estate career could be summarized as somewhat of a whirlwind. After attending university in my home town, I worked for a decade in the corporate sales world. After I did some career soul searching, my wife suggested I sell real estate for a living. I didn't object to this idea and soon after began the real estate licensing courses. Within eight months I obtained my license and got off to an exciting start, selling over one hundred homes in my first full year in the business. This is extremely rare in the real estate industry, where the average agent has perhaps four to seven transactions in the first year.

This fast success propelled me into the real estate spotlight, where I was coaching and speaking on the productivity and success I was having in such a short period of time. From the outside I appeared to be enjoying great success each and every day, however nobody knew what was truly going on inside of me. Eventually various external events began to transpire that created a very unhealthy version of myself.

Has it ever occurred to you that with the thousands and thousands of "self-help" books that probably crowd your bookshelves (I know they do mine), the focus always seems to be on helping us get further in life? More money, better relationships and improved health. Please don't misunderstand me; these are all important and noteworthy focuses. However, in my own personal journey of struggle, these kinds of books failed to offer the support I needed.

You see, while health, wealth and professional success can be critical to our happiness, it is only through the discovery of the integral-self that one can reach the realms of true joy. It wasn't until I tested (and failed) my own vow of integrity that I began to understand the truths that I know — from my own experience and that of thousands of people I've spoken to or worked with — that this is where the real work must start.

This book will allow you to discover much of your own personal integrity and guide you through a process of engaging your authentic self. From my perspective, and after many years of research, experience and a deep investigation of my own, I believe that integrity is an individual choice and discovery that is different for every single one of us.

We will also pay close attention to exploring the power of choice. What choices have you made, or are you considering making, that will quite likely hurt you or others? Have you stepped out of integrity in a relationship or had that happen to you? Do you numb your pain at the end of the day with alcohol or some other substance? We live in an addictive society, but ultimately, it's impossible to live a truly free life if we don't make choices that serve our integral-self.

Unfortunately, too many people live their entire lives without making these powerful, personal choices. Instead of discovering the truest desires of our own individual experience, most of us live in different states of existence that often do not serve us nor bring us the joy we desire.

My Own Discovery

I had very little foundation in self-help or personal development and absolutely no background in spirituality. Although I had been coached by almost every real estate training organization in the world, and with some wonderful companies in my previous sales career, I didn't know where to turn for help.

I began to work with several coaches and guides that had a spiritual element to their practices. Most of the information I was learning with them was new to me. Some of the work I began to do involved a physical transformation while other aspects covered personal growth and spirituality. All of the topics that I examined allowed me to discover more about myself.

It was the spiritual side that really resonated with me and began to impact my life. I read books on manifestation, connectivity, wholeness, astrology, energy awareness, meditation, emotional freedom techniques, healing rituals and so many more. I worked with energy healers and learned Reiki myself, and developed a deep and regular mentoring with an Ordained Minister of Metaphysics.

I spent over $100,000 on books, courses, coaches, seminars, webinars and trainers in the spiritual realm, which to this day is the best money that I have ever invested. It was far more beneficial to me than any billboard or website I had ever purchased for my real estate business.

I also began to study Universal Laws in order to develop a deeper knowing and understanding of how the manifestation process worked. Although many people dismiss these laws as they are energy based, I had a full understanding that both the Physical Laws and Spiritual Laws had applications in every aspect of our existence. They became an obsession as I wanted to understand them more deeply. I began to realize how they impacted one's relationships with people and the flow of money.

Things began to unfold. As I began to speak across North America more frequently, my coaching program became more visible and accessible inside and outside of the real estate industry. As my momentum began to grow as a real estate speaker, my client profile also began to change. Instead of brand new real estate agents looking for different ways to grow their business entering my coaching program, I began to have "Top Producers" or highly successful business people hiring me.

The irony was that they were seeking changes inside of their lives much like I had. Most hadn't yet realized that there was no amount of business success that would allow them to awaken to their own personal integrity or discover their purpose in life. Many of them had lost touch with their authentic selves, and were operating at varying levels outside of their integrity.

As my coaching client portfolio began to grow, it was surprising at first to see the vast amount of infidelity, betrayal and addiction in people's lives. Those with experiences of trauma and low self-worth frequently found that my program resonated with them. The process became one with proof to allow others to understand themselves further and begin a journey that perhaps they had not been on before. This journey allowed them to step into their own integrity more regularly and with very little resistance.

This journey is not always easy because it can be painful at times to look at your authentic self, but I assure you that with practice, focus and intention, you will awaken to a different experience each and every day.

Remember that I have been studying many of these principles for years and consistently have anchored myself to mentors, coaches and trainers who helped me stay the course. I continue to seek guidance and work with coaches and mentors to this day, as I understand it is critical to my path of awareness.

This process will support you in whatever you desire if you commit to the work. You must be willing to go deeper than the surface level of simply reading the words. I will give you some guiding principles and strategies to assist you every step of the way.

Make no mistake; this is a spiritual path to discovering greater experiences and fulfillment in life. It is a never ending journey, so I encourage you to focus on the activities involved, and detach from the results. I promise you the results will come and be grander than you would ever imagine.

It is crucial that you understand that this process works. In applying the principles I share with you in this book, I was able to transform my life in under a year, while continuing to keep my real estate, coaching and speaking businesses growing and thriving. It was when I took the spiritual path that my work became more fulfilling and my income level went through the roof. I dramatically improved my health and wellness, along with completely altering my mental state, without any prescribed medication.

I also share that I was able to take personal responsibility and begin to work on examining my own failing marriage as I had stepped out of integrity at home. This allowed me to begin a process of creating better and more meaningful relationships with my children. Although I had been *physically* present with them, I had not been emotionally present by any normal standard for quite some time.

The overview of this book can be summarized as an understandable paragraph which I'll outline below. This is really a book about the ways that people manifest and create all of their experiences. It's an understanding of why we don't create what our soul truly desires because we are often outside of our integral-selves. Often people don't understand why they make the decisions to betray loved ones or themselves. They can't stand the internal pain that they live in on a day-to-day basis, yet they keep repeating the same behaviours again and again. They often don't understand why they become obsessed or addicted in their own lives. Ultimately they haven't cultivated a relationship with their truest and most integral-self, which leads to all of these unhealthy experiences.

No matter what experience you are currently having, this book will give you a precise road map to create better experiences and manifest better outcomes. It will teach you how to engage your own authenticity and discover your integral-self.

I recommend and almost insist that you read the book in chronological order to fully utilize its potential. At the back of this book I have created a quick reference to the Universal Laws that we will explore here. There are many other Universal Laws that we do not discuss here, but I believe this book will provide great insight and a solid foundation for you getting started.

Most of us are familiar with the Universal Law of Attraction. The reason that I study all of the Universal Laws with my coaching clients is that many people do not understand the other laws thoroughly, or at all. Although they are creating or manifesting experiences, many of them are undesirable, and many of my clients initially do not understand why.

In each chapter I will ask you to journal and complete exercises in your Integrity Vow Workbook. The Workbook has been specifically designed to help you stay organized and on track throughout this process. It will outline all of the exercises in this book and has felt that anxious before. I took a pile of anxiety pills, but I couldn't calm down so I drove myself to the hospital in an absolute state of paranoia.

After I arrived and sometime in the waiting room or emergency room I must have passed out. I woke up in the state I described above, all alone. There were no friends, no family and no childhood sweetheart anywhere in sight. The doctors said I was going to be okay but gave me a very stern and sobering warning that I needed to make some changes, and make them fast. It was decision time for me. I picked myself up, dusted myself off, and I never touched cocaine or ecstasy again.

Although I got clean from drugs, I created a series of other misadventures along the way that I'll reference in this book. What I've come to understand is that each one of these experiences appeared for a reason and allowed me to evolve. It was up to me, and will always be up to me, to make the choice to create healthier outcomes.

I am grateful for this opportunity. Stepping out of integrity can occur for anyone. In my own lifetime, I have found myself stepping away from my integral-self on several occasions. My choices had an impact on my relationships, self-worth and confidence and overall capacity to evolve spiritually.

This occurred for many years until I finally came to my own realization. I had been living a giant lie and I was so sick and tired of it. Even though I had made some personal changes, I needed to make more and in a hurry. My life was falling apart and I felt so out of control again. The energy I was offering appeared to be attracting many of the same experiences.

I had been lost and feeling hopeless for quite some time. I also appeared to be stuck in a Karmic cycle which I now know was full of lessons. This had a direct correlation with the Universal Law of Cause and Effect which shows us that every action has a consequence, positive or negative.

To briefly summarize, the choices I was making were causing others to hurt and I was certainly hurting myself both physically and emotionally. I had to stop hurting myself and other human beings. There was no way around this if I wanted to live the life that I knew I could. Once again I was presented with an opportunity by the Universe to grow spiritually.

For whatever reason, I didn't adhere to the lesson that was being offered to me. I moved back and forth and around and around, constantly alternating between old patterns that weren't serving me very well. To clarify, I was spending time with the wrong people and doing the wrong things. Finally, after much more pain and suffering, I realized that I wasn't well.

I had involved myself with another woman and it was a nasty affair. I'll discuss this later in the book, but I can safely say it was the most chaotic time in my life to date.

You would think that rock bottom would have been that hospital bed, but it wasn't for me. Rock bottom was me living in fear. Rock bottom was spending time with another woman and coming home and acting like a father while wondering if I was going to get found out. Rock bottom was crying myself to sleep on my couch or smoking cigarettes in my car wondering why my life was so out of control. Rock bottom was having sex with a woman during the day and watching my wife wonder what was wrong with her marriage at night. Rock bottom was an ungrounded state of affairs that had me going sideways each and every day. Although rock bottom can be a chaotic experience for anyone, I believe that my own rock bottom centered on the fact that I was completely misaligned with my own integral-self. As we go on, I think it will become clear that anyone who feels they are at the bottom is undoubtedly living outside of integrity in some, or many, areas of their life.

Many of the great spiritual guides of our time refer to us as "artists." Don Miguel Ruiz Jr. references our journey as using a "paintbrush" to create the experience here on planet earth. For the longest time I appeared to be painting with a dirty brush. The canvas never looked very good and nobody would want to buy the art I was creating. In hindsight they were some of my most perfect creations. My paintbrush created contrast and the contrast was perfect, despite me not realizing this at the time.

I've finally come to an understanding and find peace in the process of creating each and every experience. I now know and understand that it is my own personal responsibility as the creator of my experiences. My own free will allows me to create that which I desire. This, of course, is unlike my past where I felt scared, tilted, and in some cases, paralyzed from the top of my head to the bottom of my feet.

I refer to this as darkness, and a place I needed to recognize fully. It involved a lack of integrity, drama, toxic relationships, addiction, fear, hurt and unhealthy living. It was a time and place where I consistently offered a lower vibration and attracted things to me that were vibrating at the same level.

On a positive note, I can now say that has changed. When I started to discover what my own personal integrity meant to me, I began to discover the power of making integrity-based choices. I began to realize how to create healthier choices, align with my integral-self and continually offer a higher vibration in order to create the experiences I truly desired.

I also stopped being a victim in life. I used to think that life was happening to me. The dead girlfriend, an unstable mother growing up or even a toxic affair are times when I felt the Universe was working against me. That wasn't the case at all though. As I began to take a more spiritual approach to life I began to understand that we create all of our own experiences and everything is an opportunity.

Merriam-Webster's Definition of Victim:

Definition of VICTIM

1: a living being sacrificed to a deity or in the performance of a religious rite

2: one that is acted on and usually adversely affected by a force or agent *the schools are victims of the social system*: such as *a (1)*: one that is injured, destroyed, or sacrificed under any of various conditions *a victim of cancer a victim of the auto crash a murder victim (2)*: one that is subjected to oppression, hardship, or mistreatment *a frequent victim of political attacks* **b**: one that is tricked or duped *a con man's victim*

What I came to realize was that I was in no way, shape or form a victim, but I was the one who was actually victimizing. Take a moment and reread all those traits in the above definition. They existed in me and my behaviour was the one creating the victim in others and myself. They exist in you as well.

We will continue to explore several common audiences in this book. You may resonate with one or more than one of them. First we explore those that have stepped out of a relationship, whether mentally or physically, which can often create severe consequences. Secondly we will look at those considering stepping outside of their relationships at the risk of betraying others. We will also investigate the choices that many must make when they have been betrayed, and how to explore healthier choices to navigate these circumstances. Finally we examine other experiences where many are challenged with making integrity-based decisions. This can include addictions, attachments, lack of faith in others and the misalignment with themselves. In all of our audiences, there is a consistent pattern of betraying the integral-self.

I began to understand that nobody had betrayed me in my life, and although I was acting out of integrity towards my family, the person I was truly betraying was me. Are there choices that you too must consider when it comes to your own integrity? Are you experiencing aspects of yourself that appear to be misaligned where it's creating challenges? Are you outside of your own integral-self where it's impacting others or creating a version of you that is undesirable?

I used to believe that being lost was never where I wanted to be, however my perspective has changed. I quite like the feeling now. Often when we feel as though we are lost, we are in actuality preparing for a more preferred outcome to unfold. Consider times where you were driving to a destination and deviated from the directions only to find yourself in a different and even more exciting place. The feeling of being lost has great potential and holds wonderful gifts if you seek them and try to understand them. These gifts are where you find yourself in a place of harmony and balance and catch yourself smiling for no particular reason other than being alive and well. This is the feeling of wellness, alignment and understanding what integrity means to you.

Of course this is not always an easy process and often it may sound too good to be true. This book will allow you to recognize that in our greatest challenges, gifts and evolution are present and waiting to appear abundantly for us. It is as if we've stumbled upon a room of lost treasure.

When we expose and embrace the darkness in ourselves, we can not only embrace it but also inspire others with light. I had so much darkness that I was unaware of in my own experience. The darkness that existed was brought on for many years and would creep up on me like a disease that could plague me for months or even years. The darkness could confuse me and make me question whether my reality was out of my control. The darkness could humble me and tear me down to the core where I did not know whether I could move on in this experience we call life. This darkness was always a result of being outside of my integral-self. There were no exceptions to this.

Although I continue to coach many others on the Integrity Vow process, I also work with higher level spiritual guides and mentors at all times to support my journey and continued work. I believe in the constant path of learning to support one's own life experience.

Early in my own spiritual discovery, one of my female spiritual guides said to me, "So my friend...you've made all sorts of changes, but you're not quite sure you truly want to change." I wasn't sure about anything. I was still partially lost in my own darkness and had little to no clarity on what integrity meant to me. If only I would have listened more closely to signs and signals like this at the time. If only I would have listened to my own authenticity and soul's desire.

How long could I keep up the lie I was telling others and more importantly, how long could I keep living the lies that I was telling myself? How long could I stay out of my own personal integrity and what truly served me at the highest level?

Since you are reading this book, I imagine that you too desire growth and change and have been seeking more answers. The questions that I would ask myself may be those that you are asking yourself right now. These questions are quite normal when you are outside of your integrity. You may also be experiencing lower energy which affects your vibration. I have too, which can lead to other undesirable experiences.

It was in this low vibrational state that I found I had brought myself to a new state and experience of powerlessness where I felt like there was no way out. Thankfully there is always a way out, but you must make the choice to change. I was going to make a choice to get out of this darkness or, quite frankly, I was going to destroy everything around me including other lives, my family and any sense of pride or dignity I had left. I may sound blunt but that's the truth...that's where I found myself and it was nothing but pain.

Until I realized that personal responsibility was the only way I was going to begin healing myself, I would always be moving through dark place to dark place like the lost little boy that I was. Until I understood what integrity meant to me, and determined a process to step into it for myself, I would continue on a path that was not serving me.

My hope is that this process will support you in your own journey and perhaps move you away from some of the darker experiences we can often create. It has worked for many clients that hire me for coaching.

My dark places could consist of sex, drugs, alcohol, work addiction, projects, running away from home, or even food, and none of them were much different than the other. All of these experiences were surfacing and coming to fruition for a reason. Although I didn't always realize it, I found that these experiences and feelings were not the

work, you will begin to understand how your own point of attraction impacts the experiences you are creating.

As you begin to embrace yourself and love yourself fully and completely for every aspect of who you were and who you are, you will begin allowing yourself to tap into resources and the powerful Laws of the Universe. They have always been there and always will be, which will allow you to manifest whatever choices or changes that you desire.

If some of the decisions you are currently making are not in integrity and do not feel good to you, I offer trust and hope that you will begin to understand yourself better and why you are making the choices you continue to make.

What a wonderful experience it may be for you to stop struggling with decisions you are making about the various circumstances of your life and to begin to make choices with ease. The further down this path you walk the easier the decisions will become, and a sense of knowing and second nature will gleam through you almost as if you are practicing magic. I know you may still be skeptical, but for the purpose of this book I ask that you set skepticism aside. Ask questions and seek truth not only about others but about yourself. I believe you will find your answers sooner than you think.

The vow that we make in this chapter is one of integrity. We are choosing to do the right thing in any experience we face. In my opinion it is the most important vow one can make, and one that will serve your health, happiness and well-being at the highest level possible.

I want you to take this vow for yourself and instill it into your existence. This vow, and maintaining your word and highest integrity, will serve and support you with success, once you come to understand it. Creating your own Integrity Vow is one that you create for yourself and your own unique desires. I am not simply speaking of doing right by others. I am asking you to make a vow to commit to what integrity means to you. In essence, your integrity reflects that which you desire most.

What decisions are you currently making about yourself that are not in alignment with who you truly are? Are you in a relationship that is not one of fulfillment? Do you spend time thinking about your career as a means to an end and a knowing that you could be doing something different? Are you struggling with telling the people you are close to about your sexuality? Do you feel trapped inside of your family life and marriage because you feel pressured by societal standards and the opinions of others? Are you constantly considering the thought of achieving more yet not seeing more come to fruition? Do you feel like you don't belong when you are at a social function or wonder why the next drink is so important to have a good time? These are but a few of the questions I pose as everyone has a different experience on this journey we call life.

Many of us have been acting out of integrity for so long that we would rather continue living the lie versus facing our truth and standing in our own integrity. It is not easy to stand in the integrity of the self because we must often stand alone.

Standing alone requires courage, dedication and a commitment that is one of a lifetime, and perhaps even several lifetimes, of ascension and opening. As you begin to awaken with new choices you will begin to see life through a different lens.

The challenge with living outside of our personal integrity is that it often leads to a direct correlation with our experience of others. It can lead to many different challenges such as addiction, escapism, acting out and other unhealthy choices. These can not only challenge us personally but often times they have a negative impact on those that we consider loved ones. The end result often encompasses shame, guilt and regret.

My truest belief is that we cannot love someone properly until we learn to love ourselves in the fullest and most transparent manner. Until we learn that there is nobody who will truly fulfill us and that we must let our inner love guide us into a complementary relationship, I do not believe we will be fair to ourselves or others in a relationship.

How many people enter a marriage without understanding themselves first? How many of us get involved with another human being and feel that person alone is the key to unlocking our happiness and freedom? What is it in the human experience that we feel that accomplishing the next task, securing the next job or winning the next award will make us complete? What is instilled in us from an early age that allows us to become dependent on others for love and security? Are we so programmed that we truly believe we will find happiness when we finally meet that special someone?

Looking back on my own experience before I got married I wish that there had been a course or a specific set of vows that I took before getting engaged and married to my wife. I am certain that I would have failed a test on self-love before I entered into a lifetime commitment with another human being.

The thought was not even remotely in my conscious awareness that the lack of integrity I had within myself would lead to problems, heartache and failure inside of my soon-to-be marriage.

I had no proper understanding of myself because it's not something that we learn in today's education system. We are taught English, mathematics, science and social studies, however there is not one elementary or secondary school educational program on self-awareness. Why is this?

Society has us programmed to believe that external accomplishments are necessary to create a fulfilling life. We are taught early that learning is crucial in order to create a career. We are educated to attain more schooling and degrees which will have a correlation with the amount of money that we earn and the materials we can purchase. We are consistently guided to pursue external "things" rather than exploring our inner selves.

Success is measured by these "things" and these "things" are made attractive by what society deems appropriate. In turn, this should attract a partner in life to bring us even more happiness. Do you see the problem with this yet? Do you understand just how backwards this thought process truly is inside of our system?

Consider the lives of the famous such as actors, athletes, musicians and extremely successful entrepreneurs. Mainstream media publicizes the rise and fall of many of them and glamorizes the process. We are programmed to believe that the success associated with these types of people is one to envy. We are taught that if we are so fortunate as to be given a gift or talent that situates us in the highest perceived form of success, we will have truly accomplished something in life.

The duality of this can be astounding as we also see the rise and fall of some of the most profiled and famous people in the world on a daily basis. Glamorized marriages fall apart due to the struggles of success and we see the cherished celebrity often fall from grace due to addiction, inappropriate and extra marital relationships, and sometimes even criminal behaviour. My marital situation was very similar for many years.

This also attributes to a large suicide rate in professional athletes who have a long build up to what can be viewed as a short-term career. When the career is over, the athlete does not know how to handle the "come down" and often will fall into bouts of anxiety, depression and suicidal tendency. Cases of this have been studied and documented time and time again.

The Integrity Vow is one that I believe will be a lifelong gift for anyone. It is a clear and unwavering commitment to pursue integrity of the self. If we eliminate the pressures that society places on us and understand the inward workings of our own spirit, we will allow ourselves more freedom and guidance to make the decisions that align with our own personal integrity and move away from those that do not.

This has the capacity to eliminate regret, resentment, depression, blaming, searching, and a long list of other attributes. These attributes are often associated with pursuing people, places and things that do not match our own personal truth and our deepest understanding of our own integral make up.

What if you could exchange a vow with yourself to understand your integral make-up prior to entering into an exchange of vows with another human being? Do you feel that this would support you in your understanding of yourself and others, and assist and guide you in navigating through a lifelong relationship with someone else? Do you feel that your better understanding of the self may have a direct result in a more harmonious relationship with not only your partner but perhaps the children that the two of you may co-create?

Can you consider that the initial Vow of Integrity will allow you to mend other relationships? Often that may encompass the relationships that have been challenging or have failed in the past. As you begin to understand and discover your integral-self you will often develop a compassion and empathetic energy for others. Based on my own experiences, I believe this initial vow is crucial to your creative process in life.

I outline the points of the Integrity Vow below:

I vow to discover my personal integrity. My deepest purpose is to stand in my own truth, ensuring that I am bringing my most integral-self forward into each and every experience. I understand that this vow is not one of perfection, however, it is one of application, and that I will constantly apply the vow to each and every experience I move through on this planet we call Earth.

This vow is the most important vow as it is a vow to myself to ensure I am being truthful with myself for the sake of my own well-being and spiritual growth. I cannot make this vow to anyone else other than myself as the vow is for me and me alone.

My own integrity is crucial to my well-being and it is when I understand, develop and apply this vow on a consistent basis that I will be able to enter into and embrace relationships of a personal, business or any other nature.

By making this vow, I believe I will bring forth the best I have to offer. The opinions of others will not matter, and I will move through each experience unwavering with a knowing that I am serving myself in order to serve others at the highest level possible.

I also understand that I must follow the principles of integrity in each experience I encounter, and although certain experiences may appear enjoyable to me, if they are out of integrity in any way I will distance myself and move away from them. I understand that everyone has their own personal set of vows and that they may not align with mine. With a knowing and understanding of my own Vow of Integrity, I know that I am protected and that my well-being is secure. This is Universal Law.

Take a moment and re-read this in your Integrity Vow Workbook. Sign and date it, declaring that you have chosen to step into your highest and most integral-self.

THE PROCESS

> "Attachment is the great fabricator of illusions; reality
> can only be obtained by someone who is detached."
>
> -SIMONE WELL

So how do we determine what our own integrity looks like? I assure you that it took me many years to determine a process to guide me in this.

I spent hundreds of thousands of dollars on every self-help book you could think of, on seminars, coaches and different resources, seeking answers. Finally, and after much pain and struggle, I found some answers that always existed and were readily available to me at any time for free: Universal Laws.

UNDERSTANDING UNIVERSAL LAWS

In order to determine what our own personal integrity is and to understand how we can create our ideal experiences, which is often referred to as "manifestation," a basic understanding of Universal Laws is necessary. I'm not asking you to relentlessly internalize them, but a strong understanding of the general principles will support you very well. This will allow you to begin creating the experiences you desire and deserve.

What Are They?

I want you to begin by understanding that there is a difference between the physical self and the spiritual self and therefore a difference between a Physical Law and a Universal Law. For that matter, everything in our experience has a physical component and a spiritual component.

The easiest way to describe a physical component would be to understand what we see and touch. Examples would be your car, desk, or favourite t-shirt.

These physical components work with physical laws such as the law of gravity. On the other hand, spiritual components work with what we come to understand as Universal Laws.

Spiritual components work with energy, which is something you can feel rather versus what we actually see at times. This is where integrity and alignment come into play.

The spiritual components work with Universal Laws as they are directed by energy-related aspects such as action, intention, detachment or abundance.

For a long time Universal Laws were not received well in the scientific world, however in recent years the emergence of the popular Law of Attraction began to create some momentum for these powerful laws.

The Universal Laws explain how universal energy and our spiritual components work together. Quantum physics has made many breakthroughs to continually support this and increase their validity in the scientific world.

I begin with two laws that I believe will support your initial discoveries on what integrity means to you: the Universal Law of Vibration and the Universal Law of Attraction. The reason that I bring these to your attention first is two-fold:

1. You may already have some understanding of Universal Energy and the general theory behind the Law of Attraction.
2. I believe these two laws can give you an immediate indication as to whether you are standing in your own personal integrity or not. It is an understanding of your own point of attraction. Consider this a Universal Check-In.

THE UNIVERSAL LAW OF VIBRATION

Everything in the Universe has a vibration. This law is closely tied with the Law of Attraction and should be studied well. If you can pause for a second and ask yourself what experiences you are attracting, you will begin to have additional insight.

Although physical objects have a vibration, we are able to detect vibration and observe vibration much easier in human beings. We can improve this detection as we understand our spiritual self and our personal integrity better.

Your level of vibration has a magnetic aspect to it and depending on your current experience that you are having, you may be operating with a high vibration or a low vibration.

Your level of vibration is determined by your emotional state. When you are operating from a place of fear, doubt, sadness or despair, you are operating at a lower vibration. When you are happy, clear and joyful, you are operating at a higher vibration.

What I've come to understand is that the lower the vibration that you offer, the less you will attract the positive experiences you desire and deserve. A higher vibration will attract more of what you seek and desire. This is how vibration works closely with the Law of Attraction.

I want you to begin to understand and investigate your current state of being and to uncover how your emotions are creating your current experience. As you become more and more aware of this, you will begin to understand what you are attracting.

Have you ever had really good intentions of getting something done but couldn't take the steps to get started? Do you feel guilty at times when this happens? This is common when it comes to procrastination but do you understand why you feel the way you do?

I also believe that as you begin to understand what your personal integrity encompasses, you will begin to increase your state of awareness and analyze the vibration you are offering. In doing this you will begin to work closely with our next Universal Law: the Law of Attraction.

THE UNIVERSAL LAW OF ATTRACTION

Everything that you are attracting into your life is a direct match to the energetic vibration you are offering. This is the most popular of all of the Universal Laws based on recent commercializing however it's often one that is not properly understood.

As I referenced earlier, the Universal Law of Vibration shows us that everything in the Universe vibrates as energy, therefore your emotional state is ever so important in understanding the creative and manifestation process. My purpose is to guide you through a personal understanding of your integral-self in order to create a process for shifting your emotional state which will then alter your vibrational frequency.

Many people believe that you must think about something in order to attract it. I want you to understand that the manifestation process has more to do with how you FEEL about something you want to experience.

In order to attract and create the experiences we desire, we must feel the abundance we seek versus concentrating on that which we do not have. When we do that, we are living in lack and scarcity.

If our emotional state contains lack and scarcity, this is the vibration we are offering and the outcome will be one of the same because Law of Attraction tells us that "like attracts like."

I have studied this law for years now and there is a lot of reference to "visualization" as a process to shift your perspective. I completely concur with these findings and believe that many of these visualization processes will indeed shift your perspective and begin to alter your emotional state. That being said, I believe a full self-discovery process is imperative prior to working with this law. We must understand and create a process of uncovering our own personal integrity in order to guide us to what we truly want to visualize and attract.

As we begin to move into our own integrity, and visualize what feels good to us as an individual, we will then create the emotional response that we desire, and begin to work with the Law of Attraction more effectively.

My purpose is to assist you in mastering this process in order to utilize this universal power at the highest level possible.

Moving Forward

I began to recognize that I had been manifesting and creating every experience my entire life. I began to understand that in many of these experiences I was offering a low energetic vibration and that it was creating a magnet for experiences that I did not desire.

As you move forward in your own discovery are you recognizing or exploring more of your own point of attraction? Have you begun to examine the energy you are carrying on a regular basis?

The people, places and things that I was encountering or had encountered in the past had all come into my existence based on the energy that I was offering. Some were good, some were bad, and some were downright destructive and chaotic. I had been able to manifest business success, a family, and many of the material items that I felt important to me at various times. I had also created experiences and relationships that did not serve me whatsoever that also created more chaos and even lower self-worth on my own individual journey.

Do you recognize and understand the duality here? Does this feel familiar to you in any way? I could create whatever it was that I wanted but I had not come to understand what that truly was. I had not stepped into my own integrity and aligned my emotions, energy and intentions. What a roller coaster of an experience moving from a healthy to unhealthy reality day in and day out.

It was amidst this discovery that I started to realize that I was responsible for the experiences I was creating and I was the only one that had any power to change this. I began to observe the relationships I had with others such as friends, family and consider the vibration that they were offering and what they were attracting as well.

As I continued to study Universal Laws, I began to realize that there was more to discover about myself in order to utilize the laws effectively. I began to understand how I had been programmed from an early age to have certain belief systems and internal reactive mechanisms to every encounter I had.

If I were to turn back the clock a few years, my answers would have looked much different than they do today. I was attracting people, places, things and experiences that were undesirable and unhealthy. Despite all the success I appeared to be having on the outside, I was not satisfied whatsoever on the inside. I did not know what integrity truly meant to me and I did not know why that was. I hadn't taken responsibility for anything.

What I also share is that many of my coaching clients or the wonderful human beings I work with have shared a similar series of answers to these questions. Some are highly successful business people and have wonderful families, yet they struggle with addiction. Others are among the top real estate professionals on the planet, yet they have no perspective on life's purpose and they are living in a state of emotional pain. I have clients who appear to have everything anyone could possibly want in life, however they come to my program in a state of despair as their worlds seem to be falling apart. Many of my clients have stepped out of integrity into inappropriate relationships. Others have experienced betrayal in many of their relationships from childhood to present time.

Perhaps this may sound familiar to you, and what I offer is hope. As you begin to awaken to your integral-self, and as you study your true spiritual self, you will begin to uncover the gifts that have always existed and embrace yourself for all that you are. You will begin to offer a higher vibration than ever before which in turn will attract the experiences that truly match the desires of your soul. This path of self-discovery will not be an easy one, however acknowledge yourself for starting this journey. What we celebrate tends to expand.

You may still be doubtful or apprehensive. You may be questioning or skeptical about the universal powers that exist for all of us. Some of the terms that I reference may seem foreign to you and you still may not know what integrity feels like. I promise you that like my clients and myself, by understanding yourself more deeply and at a more spiritual level, you will begin to understand all of this and step into the highest version of yourself. I'm so happy you're here.

CHAPTER 2 EXERCISES

These exercises were created in order for you to begin developing an increased sense of awareness to the energy you are offering. As you start to become familiar with and aware of your emotions, you'll begin to connect them to the outcomes they are creating.

Ask yourself the following questions:

1. What are you currently attracting into your life in current space and time?
2. What energy are you offering and what is your emotional state?
3. When you're all alone and thinking about yourself, are you satisfied with what is appearing for you?
4. Do you understand that you are personally responsible for all of the answers in questions 1-3?

Journal all of your answers in the Integrity Vow Workbook.

Trust and Violation

"Love is of the soul. Fear is of the personality."

-GARY ZUKAV

I CAN REMEMBER THE POOL of sweat, the smell of red wine and ciga-rettes, and an aroma of an unfamiliar home. I was confused and still intoxicated from the night before, however I definitely knew that I was not where I was supposed to be. In fact, I now realize that I had arrived at my own experience of rock bottom.

Although there are many facets pertaining to the definition of trust, Merriam-Webster's first point in this regard resonates with me the most:

> "*1a*: assured *reliance on the character, ability, strength, or truth of someone or something b: one in which confidence is placed.*"

In my own experience, as it pertains to my own personal vow of integrity, I believe that trust has far more to do with the self than trusting someone or something else. When we come to understand that finding our own personal integrity is where we find our own inner peace and true happiness, we begin to understand how trust in ourselves is of the utmost importance.

We also begin to understand that when we step out of our integrity and become misaligned by the choices that we make to do so, we have violated our sacred vow to stay in integrity. In essence, we have violated ourselves.

As I began to sober up and gain some clarity, I realized that I had run away from my own home the night before. It was Christmas time and I had been at a family function where I had been drinking heavily throughout the better part of the day. I had become very belligerent and irresponsible. The anxiety I was feeling made me feel very uneasy, which was a result of the alcohol, depression and lack of trust that I had created in my life.

My actions that day led to an argument with my wife which spiraled out of control and led me to leave my house. My wife had hidden my car keys, which was a blessing as I was in no mental state to drive a vehicle. I had been texting and conversing with another woman all day long. I vaguely remember leaving my house and ordering a taxi, but I knew I was going to spend time with the woman I had been having an affair with. That's where I went and where I woke up. This was not the first time I had stepped out of my integrity or broken not only my marriage vows but my vow to remain in an integral state.

I had spent the entire holiday season that year hiding out in my real estate office, fueling up on booze at night and spending most of my time manipulating my own thoughts. I wasn't present in any experience I was encountering at home or at work. I wasn't enjoying my kids as a father should during those special times, and I wasn't respecting my wife whatsoever. To say that I was in a low vibrational state and way out of my own integrity would be an understatement. I continued to try to justify my infidelity, if only in my own mind.

From the outside I may have looked like the stellar family man, but nobody knew the secret life I was living or the fear I was facing inside – that my entire world was falling apart. Nobody truly knew the choices I was making or that I had been carrying on an affair with another woman for the better part of a year. I didn't trust the man I saw in the mirror any longer. It was as if I was looking at an empty shell with hollow brown eyes of the man I once was.

My business partner and I opened an independent real estate company. It was big news in our local market and immediately gained national attention. It was exciting, relevant and what appeared to be a fantastic and exciting opportunity. It was an entrepreneurial decision for the two of us who had been working together as a sales team with a combined twenty plus years of experience. It was supposed to be the beginning of one of the most rewarding times in our lives.

It was only three days later that I received a call from a woman that I'd had a business relationship with. She did not work in my area, however she wanted to come see the office and bring a gift to celebrate the grand opening. Of course I welcomed that, as it was a nice gesture in the normal course of business and networking.

She came to the office and brought me a bottle of alcohol. I showed her around and we made small talk like we normally had in the past. There was something different from our previous interactions, however. She was a little more flirtatious than she had been in the past. She engaged me with eye contact and laughed at my jokes more than usual. I showed her around the office and we decided to have lunch at a nearby restaurant. When we departed from lunch to head back to work for the day, she made physical contact more than what seemed normal, brushing up against me and touching my hands and arms. I remember the slight feeling of fear.

We began to see each other more frequently. We talked about our goals and hopes for our different careers, our children and our lives. The duality in this was that we also often conversed about what we were lacking at home. When these conversations came up I often felt fear in those situations too. Although the conversation was masked with hope, I can now see the lack and scarcity-based vibration that we were offering to one another and to the people around us. We were breaking the trust that others had put in us by engaging in these interactions.

The relationship soon began to accelerate. The messaging frequency between her and I began to increase on almost a daily and even hourly basis. Our texts became much more flirtatious and inappropriate and finally led to direct sexual advances between the two of us. Eventually we would be the first person either of us texted in the morning, then we would text and call all through the day and be the last person each of us talked with in the evening. Although I knew that I was breaking trust and that the conversations were not integrity-based, I didn't understand why I couldn't stop. Interestingly, I can now see and recall that as exciting as the conversations were, I also felt a myriad of other emotions.

I remember the feeling of stress and overwhelm. I had never been so anxious over a relationship before. The thought of stepping out on my family made me nauseous, but the addiction to the excitement kept me engaged. I would often have to take anxiety pills to calm down after a heated sexual conversation with her.

The inappropriate photos she sent and advances she made were increasing at an exponential rate as well, which didn't help the matter. I became addicted to the experience and to my own behaviour. I didn't trust myself if I were to be in her physical presence, and I knew that deep down it didn't feel good to me. Yet I continued to carry on with her. Do you see the correlation with low self-worth here?

When I finally crossed the boundary, I had arrived home after a long weekend away. I had been away with friends at a bachelor party. Instead of spending time celebrating and enjoying the moments with my closest friends, I was consumed with texts and dialogue with her as to whether we should finally be intimate and take the relationship to the next level. We were back and forth, fighting, flirting and aggressively lusting. It's safe to say that it consumed the entire weekend. I also had a fight going on in my own mind about my intentions for this relationship and the consequences that surrounded it.

By the time I returned home from my trip I was in a state of pure panic. I was so terrified driving out to meet her at our agreed upon destination. I couldn't have stopped myself for anything back then, though.

By the time I picked her up it was a near snow blizzard outside. We drove for a few minutes and I found an abandoned driveway on a side road outside of the town we met in. We began to kiss so passionately and fiercely that I forgot about everything around me or any potential consequences. We were engulfed in one another and there was no turning back. I couldn't stop. She didn't stay long afterwards, and we both had to get home to our respective families. I cried the entire drive back.

It was the beginning of the worst two years of my existence. Of course, from a place of gratitude and reflection, I now understand that these circumstances showed up to teach me what I needed to learn about myself. It would have been ideal if the pain I created for others and myself could have been avoided, however this experience showed up for a reason.

I had violated almost every ounce of integrity I had. I had broken the trust of my family, my loved ones, but more importantly, myself. I continued this relationship by making the choice to do so and I take full personal responsibility for the outcomes I created. Although I created a lot of pain for others, I have come to terms with what I've done and found forgiveness. This was one of my life's greatest lessons and she was one of my life's greatest teachers.

This is not a new story by any means. Millions of humans are in stories of infidelity and millions will enter into inappropriate relationships this year. There is a plague that exists and one that is growing exponentially worse in the new age of social media, texting, inappropriate messaging and other means to facilitate experiences similar to the one which I created.

I also believe this is a time of great awakening in the Universe. This is a time to begin understanding how emotions can guide us to the bliss that we truly seek if we allow them to. If we awaken to our awareness and understand what our own Integrity Vow truly means, we can create a guidance system to achieve this more quickly and with ease. As we learn to trust in our own self-discoveries, we will allow others to do the same and strengthen trust in some of the relationships that do serve us well.

This lesson allowed me to take a full inventory of myself, and how I had created similar situations with the people, places and things that I surrounded myself with. Although my affair was a severe scenario, I began to recognize other situations and experiences where I was violating my own trust in myself, and in what integrity meant to me.

I share my story because it may resonate with you. Maybe you are about to enter into a relationship that will not serve you. This relationship doesn't necessarily mean one of an infidelity-based nature. Perhaps it's a business partnership, new friendship or even a family dynamic that will not truly align with your integral-self. Violating trust doesn't have to be centered on infidelity.

My decision to enter into an inappropriate relationship with another woman was one of the most chaotic experiences of my life. What began as a business relationship turned into one of the most toxic relationships I could have ever imagined creating. I was experiencing deep internal suffering and didn't know how to cope with the pain. Although time has passed, I continue to seek more forgiveness, and have since found a place of gratitude for the experience. It was also a catalyst to create the process you are reading in this book.

If we are not in a place of awareness, we cannot understand or trust our own emotions and allow them to guide us. Often times we resist this guidance, which allows other circumstances and negative energies to persist. When we allow emotions such as fear to challenge us, rather than understand what fear is, it becomes more and more difficult to make any integrity-based decisions. Remember that integrity is what we determine to be in each individual experience. Understanding fear can provide each of us with great insight into our own alignment with integrity.

In my own process I was literally living in a state of fear at all times, yet not recognizing it as a guiding force. I had stepped out of my marriage, violating the trust my wife had put in me when we exchanged wedding vows and the million "second chances" she had given me when I had screwed up before. I absolutely adored my children, and yet I was taking my family for granted each and every day by my choices to remain in an affair. I was in a constant state of war with my own integrity.

My wife couldn't make any sense of my behaviour and my children were wondering what was wrong with their daddy. My irrational behaviour, low self-worth and complete internal despair had me on an emotional roller coaster. My wife and kids didn't know if I was coming home to spend time as a family or if I was going to show up half intoxicated and moody as hell. If my wife dared make one false move or ask me what was wrong, I could turn against her in a state of rage that was completely unfair and uncalled for. I had violated the trust that my family placed in me and I was manipulating them with my actions and choices. I've now come to understand that I was also manipulating myself.

I was scared of being found out at home. I was scared of disappointing the woman I had started an affair with. And I was downright scared that I had lost any integrity that I had left in me. I knew what I was doing was wrong, and that I wasn't trustworthy. I was challenged internally as I didn't know how to trust the decisions I was making. I'd gain small moments of integrity where I felt like stopping the affair and fixing everything at home, but often I'd soon self-destruct and make plans with the woman I was seeing. I was confusing everyone around me, including the person I had the affair with, but more importantly I was continually confusing myself.

As I've come to understand what integrity means to me, and as I continue to assist others in a discovery process of their own, I am certain that one of the most important aspects of creating the experiences we desire is to understand trust.

It is a very crucial aspect of the manifestation process when we work with the Law of Attraction to understand the following: the trust I discuss here is not as much about how people perceive the trust they can place in others, rather it is the trust we understand and live by in our own experience. It is the trust that we place in ourselves to make healthy and self-serving choices. When we violate this trust, we are often then working in cause and effect, which shows us that every action has a reaction or a consequence.

It was not until I understood that I had to learn how to trust myself, and allow my awareness and intuition to guide me, that I began to make choices to regain my own personal integrity. I had to feel the fact that kissing my wife goodbye in the morning and then kissing another woman goodnight in the evening was a complete violation of trust to all parties.

It was in those moments I began to realize the energy I was offering to everyone around me, and that I had to place trust in my intentions to redirect that energy to my own personal integrity. I could no longer worry about anyone around me or how they felt about my untrustworthy behaviour. I had to find it for myself and step into it on my own. It was like I had to learn to trust myself for the first time in my life.

Let me explain that although I finally ceased all contact with the woman I was seeing, I don't blame her for any of the experiences that I created with her. They were my own decisions and choices and I take full personal responsibility for those experiences. Violating my own trust and integrity allowed me to violate the trust she had in me as well. Nobody deserves to feel hopeless and sick, and both of us had stepped out of our integrity, causing an unhealthy state of being for each of us in our own way.

Of course based on the Universal Law of Attraction that we discussed previously, there was good reason why we decided to enter into this type of relationship. In essence, we were offering very similar energy to the world, and we attracted one another naturally. That's just how it works. I was her and she was me. Sounds strange, I know, but I promise you'll understand more as you read on and discover for yourself. We are all on different journeys, however the lack of trust and integrity we both had at the time created a point of attraction between us and in turn violated the trust that others had placed in us.

It was a very challenging time for both of us as I do believe we felt the feeling of love towards one another. Of course, I've come to understand that I could not have loved her or anyone including my family properly, as I was not loving myself properly on any level.

In Gary Zukav's book *The Heart of The Soul* he delves deeply into the topic of Emotional Awareness and how energy enters and exits our bodies as love and trust or fear and doubt. As I reflect back on this experience I know that almost every decision I was making over that two-year period was fear-based and there was very little love that was truly involved at all.

The crucial aspect of understanding how energy and emotions enter and exit our body allows us to utilize these gifts and feelings as a guidance system. You can literally begin to understand your own energy in each and every moment, and ask whether or not you feel your integral-self or something else. As you begin to gain certainty as it pertains to your own integrity, you will begin to trust in this emotional guidance system even further.

I began to study Karma and how the Law of Cause and Effect was working in my life. Negative Karma was showing up front and center in the circular manner it always does. I also began to study Dharma which is more of a linear and purposeful nature. I began to make the choice to work more closely with Dharma, which also places an emphasis on serving our families and purpose. It had seemed like a nightmare that lasted for years, however I was finally waking up and beginning to trust myself again.

Interestingly, my home life hadn't been that bad to begin with. My wife is a very attractive woman, my three kids are amazing, and we were all very involved in their activities and sports. I always took joy in those moments and in the one-on-one time I spent with my wife when we made the time. Although our marriage wasn't perfect, we enjoyed our friends and family and had very little to complain about. There was something I continued to recognize about my marriage throughout the entire affair, even when I acted out. I don't know how to describe it exactly, but I felt that my wife and I had unfinished business, and that gave me the sense of hope.

You will begin to find out what your own integral-self means in its truest form. You will also begin to understand how to discover the choices and decisions you are making in regards to your own integrity. You will keep the commitment to your own integrity vows front and center. As you discover your own integral-self further, you will begin to trust the process and all of the decisions that pertain to it.

I'm so excited for you and your journey. The gifts that your own Integrity Vow holds will serve you on a level you may have yet to experience. As you gain confidence and clarity, you will begin to trust every decision you're making and how it pertains to your own well-being. You will begin to allow yourself to consistently raise your own vibration and point of attraction for the experiences that you desire. My greatest advice to you in this understanding is to trust in the process. As you trust in the process, even if it's a borrowed belief for the time being, you will begin to trust yourself again and again and again. Little by little, you will gain more and more clarity in your own personal experience.

You will also begin to learn more about the Universal Law of Association, which indicates that we become like the five people we surround ourselves with most. If you write your five down, I believe you will find great answers in that discovery. This will serve you even further.

As you begin to understand yourself further, you may experience moments when it is challenging to keep your commitments. I assure you that this is normal for everyone. The key is to remain committed. Often times we resist the gifts that are presented to us as it can be extremely painful to look inside of ourselves. In keeping your commitment to the self-discovery process in this book and beyond, you will begin to trust in the decisions you make more and more.

As you move further down your own path of integrity, you will also begin to allow all of your emotions to guide you from an intuitive level. As you increase your state of personal awareness, you will continually open your intuition further. Understanding emotions such as fear will become a great aiding gift to you, and you will continually trust your intuition.

So why don't we allow these gifts to simply guide us with ease? What is it in us that resists the gifts that are available to each and every one of us? Let's look at the Universal Law.

THE UNIVERSAL LAW OF RESISTANCE

This law indicates that anything offering resistance will create or manifest more of the same. This means blocked energy, and it is a challenging law to understand. We all face this at different times in our life, however recognizing and embracing it will ease some of the difficulties we experience.

More often than not, we find ourselves using this law on an unconscious level. Often times we are not familiar with it or aware that it is occurring.

We now understand the Universal Law of Attraction in that like energy attracts like energy, similar to a magnet. Understanding the Law of Resistance is important, as the energy we attract is often one of a consequential or negative nature.

Negative energy often creates more of the same, and this can result in various blockages, along with the manifestation of illness, both mental and physical. The more resistant we are to certain outcomes, the more we create these blockages.

To put things into perspective, I was resisting the outcomes of having an affair and making integrity-based decisions. I did not trust the choices I was making, and I continued to violate my own sense of integrity. As I continued to resist my inner truth, I continued to attract more of this negative energy. It began to create illness inside of me, both physically and emotionally. Do you see how this works?

I had allowed this energy to situate itself in my experience, and rather than allowing my guidance system to move me to a more integral-based and positive direction, I kept resisting and creating more and more negative outcomes.

I was so resistant to adapting to the natural flow of the Universe and what my integrity was truly telling me to do, that I created a situation where I felt very stuck. This was the energy that had parked itself on my doorstep.

What I began to learn was that understanding and trusting my emotions could guide me in a better direction. What I needed to grasp was that there was a reason I was experiencing so many of these emotions in the first place.

I began to understand myself better, and through the coaches, mentors and studying I was doing, I started learning about myself in great detail. I began to realize and self-discover what was creating these experiences in the first place.

This book will allow you to do the same.

CHAPTER 3 EXERCISES

This chapter examines trust so the exercises are designed for you to explore areas where trust in others and yourself may have been compromised throughout your life.

1. Journal five experiences that you have created where you did not trust the decisions you were making at the time. They can be as simple or as complex as you like.
2. Journal five experiences that you have felt like someone behaved in an untrustworthy manner towards you.
3. For your answers to Exercises 1 and 2, I'd like you to journal about the feelings that you associate with those experiences. Be as descriptive as possible.
4. For your answers to Exercises 1 and 2, journal how you created each of these experiences and take full responsibility for the outcomes. Journal how you feel, being as descriptive as possible.

Control

"The reason many people in our society are miserable,
sick, and highly stressed is because of an unhealthy
attachment to things they have no control over."

-STEVE MARIBOLI

I WAS BEGINNING TO COME to terms with the fact that my marriage
was falling apart. This was mentally crippling to think about as we
had three young boys at home and a whole bunch of responsibilities.
More importantly, I felt as though I had given up on the one person who truly didn't deserve to be given up on, which was my wife.
She had been there for me through everything and despite all the
nonsense and negative experiences I had created, she always found a
way to forgive me and work things out. I wasn't sure I'd ever forgive
myself for violating her trust.

I did not feel that I was being fair to my family or staying in
integrity at home. I felt that I would be a better father and man if I
left my home and sought out the relationship I had become addicted
to. What a sad state of affairs I had created and I couldn't stop myself
at the time from carrying on down the dark path of my affair. I had
let it take control of me.

The very last time the woman I was having an affair with and
I were intimate, we were intoxicated, and for whatever reason she

mentioned being intimate with another man just moments after we had slept together. I could feel it in my soul that this was a toxic relationship and that we were attempting to control each other's emotions. When we try to influence another's emotions by bringing forth feelings of insecurity or jealousy, we are seeking some kind of control.

Right there in that moment it hit me. I realized that I was in the wrong place with the wrong woman and that this was never going to get better. Our relationship was never going to improve or evolve into something more meaningful. I had lost all integrity and control of my mind and I needed to get the hell out of there. I couldn't just leave as I had spent about twelve hours drinking and was too intoxicated to drive. I didn't say anything about wanting to go because she could be very volatile and I wasn't prepared for a scene. I eventually passed out, but in the early morning hours, around 4:00 a.m., I woke up in a cold sweat. It was time to regain control of my life.

Perhaps you are having similar moments when your intuition and energy are trying to tell you something. Are you in a relationship that no longer supports your well-being and integrity that you must remove yourself from? Have you experienced betrayal and are you unsure as to what your next steps are to resolve or leave a relationship? Do you have other circumstances where clear signs and signals are guiding you to a knowing that change is in order? You may not have the answers yet, but pay attention to the signs and you will more and more begin to realize what direction you need to take. Remember to reflect and write in your Integrity Vow Workbook. This process will assist you in your discovery.

I didn't know what to do, but all I wanted was to go home. It wouldn't be pretty, and my wife would likely question where I was for the night, but I needed to be there. I had to be in a place where I felt safe.

I jumped in a taxi and went to my office to shake off some of the cobwebs from the night before. I cleaned myself up and went home. I felt as though I had no power over what was going to happen, but that I could make an excuse to my wife as to why I hadn't come home the night before. Once again I was trying to control the outcome of the circumstances I had created. I didn't realize that I had no control over the outcome of this experience, yet something felt familiar.

I grew up in the city where I live now. My parents divorced when I was three years old. It was not a nice divorce, not that any of them are really. My mother was bipolar and my father and I did not have a relationship from the time that I was eight until I turned twenty. Between the ages of three and eight I would see my father sporadically in the typical every other weekend custody arrangement. I remember the hostility my mother showed whenever he would pick me up for a weekend. She would not refrain from yelling, swearing or becoming physically violent with him in front of me.

Due to this unhealthy and horrifying behaviour, and based on the recommendations of the courts and family psychologists, my father had to remove himself from my life when I was only eight years old. The hostility and violence always worsened and the threat of my mother becoming emotionally unstable was constant. There was the possibility that she could take her own life, his life, mine or any combination of the three. She had an ability to manipulate just like I do, and she was able to manipulate the court system.

Although I did have other men in my life when I was young, I had very few who I would consider good male role models or points of reference. My mother dated other men when I was growing up, but the relationships never turned out very well. It was a normal occurrence to witness her physically attacking men, family members or friends, and ultimately while I was still at a young age she started verbally and physically abusing me. I recall a mix of emotions as a child. I could find myself afraid of her at one moment, then feeling like a normal child and sometimes even jealous of the relationships she entered into. Let's just say it was a roller coaster ride of a childhood.

As a young boy and only child I didn't understand what was considered "normal" behaviour or what was not. I did not realize that being hit, strangled, slapped in the face or chased around a house with knives and baseball bats was any different from what other children were experiencing. Powerlessness became the norm.

You don't realize what this does to your self-esteem as a young child. You don't get to learn what's normal. Whether it was growing up without a father or having a mother who was physically and verbally abusive, you don't understand what life might be like without that chaos. You have no control over this at such a young age. You also don't understand the negative charge it creates that can stay with you for years, or perhaps lifetimes. Unconsciously, experiences like this can manifest as inner programming without you even knowing it.

I realize this paints a horrific picture, however I want to clarify that my childhood also had some positive experiences. I always had decent clothes and toys, played sports and went on holidays. I excelled in school as a child, was pretty good at any sport I played, and even became the captain of the high school football team.

There was, however, lots of trauma in those early years. I remember many nights when I was eight or nine years old when I would be at home, alone and afraid. My mother was working shift-work as a nurse and often times she couldn't afford a babysitter. I would hear the sounds a house makes and wonder if someone was hiding inside. Many nights I fell asleep feeling frightened.

I can still remember one of the vacations I went on with her. I was walking through a hotel hallway to get ice from an ice machine and another kid staying in the hotel came up to me and asked if I was okay. His family had heard me screaming from outside our hotel room. I'm not sure what it was that I did to provoke it, but I can still remember the fear I felt when my mother attacked me.

She was screaming and yelling and had picked up a toy gun that I had received at Disney World that day. It was a pirate musket style gun made with real wood. She was swinging the gun at me, threatening that she was going to kill me. I tried everything in my power to block the gun from hitting my face. There was nothing that I could do in this situation as my mother was a grown adult and I was just a little boy. I can still feel the terror to this day. I can feel the big wooden gun handle sweeping in front of my face as I cried and begged her not to hit me. That gun was heavy enough that it could have killed a child if it had hit me, and it came close in the way she was swinging it. It was one of the most terrifying experiences of my life. It was both abusive and traumatic.

These powerless situations in which I had no control were not always of a physical nature. Watching her berate someone at a store or in a restaurant was always uncomfortable and embarrassing. She did not know how to cope with her illness or the responsibilities of raising a child.

There were also moments of abandonment that clearly left me feeling powerless. I recall being in an argument with my mother at a shop in a beach town when I was eleven years old. It was about a twenty-minute drive from where we were actually vacationing and I had been misbehaving for not getting what I wanted at one of the stores. When my mother finally lost her temper, she dragged me out of the store yelling and screaming at me. I can literally remember my feet leaving the ground as she pulled me by my shirt. There were people all around us, and you could tell that many of the other patrons were quite concerned. Some were confronting her asking her to stop, saying things like, "That is no way to treat a child!"

I just wanted it to stop. It was embarrassing and scary at the same time. When she finally stopped, she got into her vehicle and drove away, leaving me behind. She left me alone for almost two hours, which was beyond frightening. This was another childhood experience that led to a feeling of helplessness.

The coaching process I facilitate and principles in this book pay close attention to how your current experiences have been created. Exploring moments of trauma, abuse, abandonment or specific low self-worth areas is of utmost importance. It is when you uncover and learn from these experiences that you will allow yourself to utilize them as gifts. This is often challenging as often the experiences are buried deep within the unconscious mind.

I did not realize at the time that all of these experiences would become incredible gifts to evolve from in my lifetime. I did not realize that I would have to go backwards at some point in my life to make amends with these circumstances. I did not realize that these childhood experiences would continue to occur in varying degrees time and time again. I certainly had no idea that there was Karma associated with them.

They would continue to affect the way that I experienced life until I found resolution with them. Until I was able to claim my own power for myself and face my fears and past programming, the same types of situations seemed to reoccur. The relationships that I would have with childhood friends, girlfriends, family members and co-workers would all end up mirroring the experiences that I had in childhood. They would all hold the same lessons and some of them would be more traumatic than others. Each of them showed up to teach me about control.

I was responsible for creating my own experiences and yet I was trying to control everything outside of me. This was a point of attraction for me to begin to create similar experiences time and time again.

Pause for a moment and consider what your current experiences are and whether you can examine past experiences and how they relate to your current reality. Are you in an inappropriate relationship and do you feel as though you are out of control? Are you considering stepping outside of your integrity and feeling you are losing control of yourself? Have you experienced circumstances inside or outside of a relationship that you feel you have no control over, such as an addiction?

I'm not asking you to determine all of your answers right now. What I am asking you to feel is a familiarity that may have occurred in the past. You will begin to walk backwards and visit other experiences to explore where you may have been seeking control or lost control. They will occur in relationships and memories, usually from early childhood. Take a moment and journal some of your experiences that resonate with you on this topic in your Integrity Vow Workbook. A constant reflection on how every experience shapes our current reality is an absolute in the work we will do together.

Bullying is epidemic in our society, and despite all of the anti-bullying strategies bullying is now more prevalent than ever in the online social world. Children are having their confidence completely stripped at early ages with the ongoing use of social media.

I was often bullied in school about my mother, along with the fact that I was an overweight child. My mother had no boundaries on when she might act out, which included her showing her anger in front of my friends. It was embarrassing and created even lower self-worth in me when she behaved this way. My friends would sometimes tell me that their own parents forbade them to come to my house.

Between my circumstances at home and the school yard, the powerlessness left me defeated and lonely. I then began a journey of self-destructive habits to numb my pain and seek out validation from others. It wasn't until my teens that I began to shift away from this compromising position through the use of violence. Essentially violence has everything to do with trying to control others and has no integrity to it whatsoever.

I always found myself in fights on the school ground. By the time I hit my mid-teens I was drinking alcohol on a regular basis. Fighting became the norm for me. I liked the feeling of being able to make someone submit with fear or to overwhelm them. It became part of my identity at the time. I remember as a kid that parents, teachers and coaches would say I was fighting for "attention." I didn't agree at the time, but I do now. I understand that I was continuing the vicious cycle I was brought up in. I was attempting to control others with violence. I am so incredibly grateful I have not allowed this negative cycle to continue with my own children.

As I've come to understand this further, I also now know that I was seeking validation from others, and fighting was a way to try to control the opinions of my peers. In essence, I was also trying to control my own mind with a false premise of validation. Validation only lies within and this was nothing more than a toxic replacement for self-worth.

I created these experiences time and time again throughout my teens and young adulthood. Whether it was substance abuse, violence, inappropriate relationships or even workaholism, I was trying to control everything I was experiencing outside of myself. The patterns continued to repeat themselves time and time again until I realized I needed some guidance and help. Perhaps you feel the same way as I did in that I was completely out of control.

I needed help in the worst way and I needed some guidance on how to better understand myself. I needed to learn why all of these experiences kept appearing in my life. I needed to find my own strength and control my own experiences rather than trying to control something or someone else. I had done therapy both individually and with my wife. None of it worked for us. I had read some marital and self-help books, but those didn't seem to have any long-term effect either.

Through the industry I work in, I was eventually introduced to a personal development coach and several other spiritual guides. When I was working with these people, they often discussed balance, integrity, energy and self-serving behaviour among other topics that resonated with me such as control and power.

One of my first mentors had a strong presence in the real estate industry I worked in, however he took a different approach to coaching, placing a stronger emphasis on personal development. I told him about my company, success and background, and within the second call I believe I told him that I was having an affair. He didn't go deeply into that right away, however.

He asked me about my health. I had been overweight as a kid and was overweight when he first started coaching me. To clarify, I was thirty-seven years old, five foot nine and 197 pounds of fat with a little bit of muscle. I had tried working out with trainers for years and had tried doing it on my own too, but it never lasted very long. He brought this to my attention. He asked me what I thought it was inside of me that I could not commit to it. Much of the process in the work I did with him revolved around this.

I began working out regularly and it seemed to put me in a slightly better mood. He suggested a nutrition plan and I began to follow it and actually saw results. I decided to do a ninety-day non-toxic cleanse. I even decided to give up alcohol for ninety days, which I didn't think would last.

My wife didn't think I would make the ninety days either. She encouraged me, but after ten years of going back and forth, destroying birthdays, holidays and special times, and vowing I would not drink again, she had no reason to believe I could stop for a week, let alone ninety days. She didn't know how much pain I was in, though. I needed something to latch onto like never before.

As I reflect about the original work I began with my own guides and coaches, it started as a way for me to seek help, but also to position myself away from the woman I was having an affair with. It allowed me to increase my own self-worth which was something I did have control over, and I assure you that you do too. I am grateful for these experiences and special humans as they also gave me a borrowed belief that making healthier choices was quite possible in my own experience.

How about you? As you read this book, I want you to begin to identify the areas that you desire change in the most. Continually reflect and journal in the Integrity Vow Workbook on what it is that you desire to change. Take an inventory of yourself in three areas to start including your body, mindset and spiritual growth. Where do you feel that change is needed most in order to impact all of your experiences?

As I reflect, I can also admit that much of the work I originally did was of a manipulative nature. I was beginning to step into my own integrity, however I was still seeking to control the opinions of others from a validation standpoint. This included the woman I had the inappropriate relationship with.

I was so out of control and seeking to control her circumstances because I wanted to show her just how good I was. I wanted to make her pay for all of the pain she had caused me. I couldn't believe that another human being could treat someone the way that she had treated me with all of her lies and deceit. Tell me that wasn't the pot calling the kettle black!

At the time, I hadn't taken any personal responsibility for my actions or for stepping out of my own truth and integrity. Through the personal work I had begun to do, I came to understand what true responsibility means and how it applies to every choice and decision we make in our lives.

I began to see life through a different lens, one where I got to take responsibility for every choice I had made in the past, and every choice I was making on a day-to-day basis. I began to question every decision I was making, whether it was business, family or personal in nature.

I also started investigating what may be considered ego-based decisions versus spiritual or self-serving decisions. I began learning about how I had been programmed in my early years, along with learning about masculine and feminine energy. The ego will always exist, but I was being taught to bring forth my feminine energy which would help me in spaces such as grace and gratitude.

This was so challenging at the start because I had spent so many years making choices based on trying to gain control of what was going on around me. I had to journey inwards further to find what had created all of these outcomes. I had to determine why it was that I behaved the way that I did. I soon discovered that much of it had to do with two things: power and powerlessness.

As I began to self-discover and learn much about the powerful Universal Laws, I started to realize how little control I actually had over external circumstances. I fully realized why I had come to such a state of powerlessness in my relationship with the woman I was having an affair with. I began to understand the point of attraction which brought us together in the first place, and that I would need to redirect my energy with intention in order to make better choices and remove myself further. I could no longer seek to control her behaviour or question her motives and involvement with me.

I could also no longer numb my feelings of low self-worth or lack of integrity by increasing my workload or using alcohol. As we discussed in previous chapters, both of these would continue to keep me in a low vibrational state, which in turn would attract more of the same experiences I was trying to eliminate.

The woman I stepped out of my marriage with was not pleased when I decided to end our affair. I felt sorry for her and wanted to help her nonetheless, as a friend. Even when we were not speaking, I was seeking to control the situation. I was seeking to find out what she was doing by watching her social media, driving by her home or calling her from a blocked number. Although I thought I had come a long way, I realize now that I was still hoping to control her. This would prove to be impossible.

Looking back, this was so incredibly foolish of me. I had ended the affair, however I felt that I could help her. Who was I to help anyone when I couldn't help myself? I had no control over her circumstances or decisions. She was on her own journey. The more I tried to help, the more she resisted or self-destructed in her own ways. It was out of my control, and I had to let go.

This wasn't easy at the start. There were times when I saw her in a state of panic over the divorce she was going through or the challenges she was facing in her personal life. There were times that she threatened to take her own life, and there were other sad moments where her emotional overwhelm brought her to her knees and her own rock bottom. I recall seeing her drop to her kitchen floor in panic, crying and apologizing profusely to me. As much as I tried to help, I had to let go of my own controlling behaviour. Even though I was stepping into my own integral-self by not having a physical relationship with her, it was time to realize that all contact had to cease and my energy had to be directed elsewhere. This would require a dedication to control my own thoughts and emotions.

Control is but an illusion. Ultimately the only thing that we can control is ourselves, and that is something that less than five percent of the planet's population knows how to do. This is the ultimate discovery for all of us. How do we give up control over trying to change external circumstances? We must in order to gain maximum internal power and to start understanding the power that lies within each and every one of us.

I completely understand that this is not an easy process, but I assure you that once you learn it, it will change your entire experience. This lesson is one that we must constantly commit to as there are experiences that will show up to shift us back out of our integrity. Personal awareness is crucial and so is the commitment to integrity.

My purpose here is to move you into a place of action where you begin to determine what control means to you and how it affects your integral-self. This is a process of identifying where the experiences you're having today originated from in the past. It's the process of walking backwards to find them, and what you may need to find resolve with. Reflection and self-examination will be a part of cleansing and clearing various aspects of yourself that do not support your integrity.

I had to walk backwards to revisit the experiences that I hadn't come to terms with. I discovered many similar experiences that had to do with abandonment, low self-worth and powerlessness. It was painful to do some of the work required here as it is often painful to look at ourselves. This was the recognition and discovery of how I had created my current reality, and it was the most soul searching I have ever done.

Many of my coaching clients enter into my program because they feel they have lost control over their time inside of their busy careers. In every single case there was always an underlying issue that had more to do with choices than time. What I am seeking to assist them in discovering is that we all have one hundred and sixty-eight hours in every week, and it is the choices that we make inside of that time where we all have complete control. As it was taught to me and as I continue to teach others, it's not about time management, rather it is about *choice* management.

More importantly, my clients soon discover that they have control over all of the choices that they are making, however they must take full personal responsibility for each and every one of them. They must begin to control their thoughts and direct their energy with intention to the exact experiences that they would like to create. They must choose the integral-self.

Often times they become frustrated as they do not understand why they cannot make proper choices both inside and outside of business. This discovery is such a blessing as it opens the door to the personal path of awareness which of course, with the right choices, will move them straight into integrity.

The process I have them follow is one I have learned well and discussed a great deal in this chapter. We can examine what we are experiencing in current space and time. We can create an ideal outcome as to what we hope to experience in the future, which in my own deepest truth is happiness and freedom.

Sounds easy, right?

You must come to understand that the Universal Law of Cause and Effect has much to do with what you are currently experiencing. Remember that every action has a reaction or consequence, whether positive or not. It is crucial to discover some of the reactions that we have had to past programming and past experiences.

To provide my own example: I identified the current experience I was having in regards to the affair. I explained I had no control over the situation other than to direct my energy elsewhere, immediately moving into a healthier state. It was my thoughts and emotions I had to regain control over. In order to do so I had to rediscover and investigate other experiences I had encountered. Some of these included violence, bullying, abuse and my childhood experiences that had created places of powerlessness that I had no control over at the time.

When we walk backwards into our past, we ultimately seek to connect to the inner child and ultimately the divine spirit. Often this will allow you to learn more about Karma, which is circular in nature. The reactions and consequences that are created from our past experiences often show up in our current ones. It is crucial for you to understand the thoughts and emotions that are associated with past programming and experiences as well. We hold energetic charges to these experiences, and often they are negative. These are often referred to as energetic cords.

The negative thoughts and attitudes that appear in our life such as jealousy, resentment, anger, and sadness are Karmic signals. They appear to teach us that we still have incomplete experiences to resolve. The circular nature of Karma means that they will continue to appear over and over again until we find and dissolve the energy associated with them. This requires a deep-rooted cleansing of the soul, and is a sacred path to happiness and freedom. It requires awareness, discovery, rituals, and the invoking of grace and gratitude which I'll discuss later in this book.

One of my coaching clients came into my program displaying a frantic pursuit of success. When he first began, I could not understand the original cause of such a fanatic way of doing business. After three calls, he sent me a picture of himself from a day before with black eyes and a fat lip. His partner was beating him on a regular basis. He had no intention of leaving the relationship, however he was avoiding the emotions attached to it by continually seeking to escape inside of his career.

As he began the path of self-awareness, he quickly identified that the relationship he had with his father was almost identical to the relationship he was currently experiencing. The years of physical abuse that he had encountered appeared over and over again in his other relationships. His point of attraction was appearing in every relationship he created. He had continued to hold onto a negative charge from the relationship with his father, and the effects continued to surface time and time again.

When he began to dissolve the Karma associated with his father through forgiveness, he began to identify what a good relationship felt like to him. He stepped into his own integrity and ended the abuse from not only others, but the abusive nature of himself. He no longer escaped into work, but began to use it as a vehicle to enjoy healthier relationships and life, and to create a better sense of purpose.

Happiness and freedom are right around the corner for you. The process of investigating your past programming is not an easy one and often times it brings forth a lot of pain that may be buried in your unconscious mind. Often times the pain is so severe that it's too difficult to experience it and we escape into even more past programming. Unfortunately, this doesn't work.

There is a solution though, and you are on your path of discovering it. You are beginning to understand the powerful Universal Laws that will aid you in attracting more and more of the experiences that you desire and deserve. You are beginning to understand yourself further as you move down your own path of awareness, finding your integral-self and alignment. The path of examining your own authenticity is not always an easy one, but amazing things await you.

CHAPTER 4 EXERCISES

The purpose of these exercises is for you to become familiar with experiences where control was present. When you come to understand that the only things you can truly control are your own thoughts and actions, you will make substantial progress towards what you wish to create.

1. Journal five experiences you have encountered when you have felt that you had little or no control. Write down how you felt during those experiences in as much detail as possible.
2. Journal five experiences you have encountered when you have felt that you had complete control. Write down how you felt during those experiences in as much detail as possible.
3. Where in your current journey do you feel that you are having experiences that are out of your control and that you would like to change? Journal your answers and how you feel about each one.

CHAPTER 5

Addiction

"Not feeling is no replacement for reality. Your
problems today are still your problems tomorrow."

-Larry Michael Dredla

I HAVE BEEN CHALLENGED WITH addiction. I have been the addict who
knows no limits and does not set proper boundaries. I have been the
addict who will continue to seek a numbing feeling in any way I can
because I do not want to face this pain alone. I have been the addict
who will prey on you if you are what I so desire. I have been addicted
to people, places and things. I was often times obsessive.

It took me a long time to embrace this part of myself. When I
began to understand it, I began to set myself free. I am still challenged with an addictive personality, however I now seek freedom,
alignment and integrity. They are clearly better choices for me.

What about you?

Perhaps there is a specific addiction that you are facing challenges
with and do not know how to overcome. Is there a substance, circumstance or another person that you've become addicted to? Have
you entered into a relationship with a person, place or thing that
does not support your integral-self? It is not easy to explore and

come to terms with any of the above, but transparency in this is crucial in your evolution.

I remember the first time I tried cocaine quite well. I was in my early twenties and so nervous about trying it. I snorted one line without getting much of a buzz. I later decided to try it again and it gave me a little more of a high. Gradually I started doing the few odd lines when I'd go out with friends.

Fast forward about six months and I was buying two or three eight balls a night, each time I went out for an evening of socializing. An eight ball is one eighth of an ounce or three and half grams. Picture a large heaping tablespoon of white powder like flour. I could comfortably say that on my own I was doing two to three grams of coke a night on the weekend, and usually a night or two during the week. Coming down off the high of cocaine is a painful experience and the big binges were never fun when they ended.

This could include horrendous periods of short-term depression or anxiety. I would have to take anxiety pills just to calm down most of the time. For several years I had been taking prescription anxiety pills from my doctor, such as clonazepam. Originally I had started taking these for ongoing bouts of anxiety, and they too are considered highly addictive. One drug would take me up, and another would bring me down. It was a vicious cycle. It was a place that I recall remorsefully, as the internal pain I was experiencing was profound. I was the one creating more of the negative feelings, but I couldn't see that then.

One of the times I'd woken up in the hospital I didn't know how I'd even arrived there. To my own disbelief, this was the third time in six months that I had been in a hospital and the second time that I had woken there. Both times I woke up there I was totally alone. The first time had been several months before. I was out drinking and doing drugs when my rowdy group of friends and I got in a bar brawl. I woke up hung over, had a friend drive me to the hospital and they immediately performed surgery on my broken hand. I wish I had the chance to apologize to whoever I hit that night. I was a different person then, and if that pain caused them any physical or emotional harm, I am truly sorry.

The second time I had been to the hospital was another self-induced choice to be reckless. I had partied for a few days, primarily on ecstasy, and when the partying stopped I started having unbelievable bouts of panic attacks. I didn't understand anxiety at the time or how overwhelming it can be. I would experience a rapid heart rate, dizziness, nervousness and depression. Anxiety attacks are horrific because you feel like you may be having a heart attack or dying, even though it's all just an illusion in your head.

The doctors even plugged me into an ECG machine, which indicated I was fine. They were monitoring my heart activity and although they indicated I would be ok, they advised me to stop the drug use. I didn't listen to them at the time, nor did I listen to myself. Although I had a drug addiction, my real addiction was to low self-worth.

Waking up alone in a hospital not even knowing what happened or having a faint recollection of the circumstances that got you there is an unbelievably dark feeling. It also identifies several things:

1. You have done something to yourself or been involved in a situation that literally took you to a hospital. This is never good.
2. You're going to have to talk to someone about whatever happened even if you don't plan on taking anyone's advice on the matter.
3. You are alone.

It took me three visits to the hospital but gradually I began to see the lessons involved with my destructive behaviour. Every experience shows up to shape us. It allows us the opportunity to learn, grow and evolve from every situation if we make the choice to do so. These were also pivotal moments when I began to understand my own integral-self.

Not all of my clients experience severe forms of addiction such as these. However, in almost every case, each of us has aspects of low self-worth we often become addicted to. This can involve infidelity, betrayal or any other circumstance where we find ourselves addicted to self-destructive behaviour.

When I eventually learned my lesson that drugs were not going to create the experiences I desired, I made the choice to stop. It wasn't horribly difficult for me, however I began to find replacement addictions and seek out other forms of pleasure.

In elementary schools we learn that cigarettes, alcohol and marijuana are "gateway" drugs that often lead to other drug use. I believe this to be true; however my hope is that the education system focuses more on why we experiment with drugs in the first place. What are the underlying causes for people to make the choices that potentially cause them harm? Nonetheless we live in a society that embraces the legal use of alcohol, and in some cases the legal use of marijuana, and this doesn't appear to be changing anytime soon.

I got drunk for the first time when I was thirteen years old. It was the summer that I was heading into high school and at that time I had been spending a lot of my summers at my cousins' house. As a kid I had three cousins that I was very close to, who lived about thirty minutes away from me in a small town of two thousand people. It was an escape from my own home at the time, and I loved going there.

My two older cousins were far more experienced than my youngest cousin and me. We would follow the older ones around or tag along, play fight and get into normal kid trouble, all while having a good time.

As I grew older, my two eldest cousins began to transfer some of their experiences to me. They taught me about women, partying, drugs and alcohol long before I ever even knew what they were. Every time I went to their house I'd hear stories of drinking or fighting or one of them having an experience with a female. I remember seeing nudity on the TV for the first time when I was there. My aunt and uncle were incredibly good people, but they didn't pay much attention to what we were up to. They figured boys were just boys. My cousins also taught me how to fight and how to stick up for myself using violence. My cousins introduced me to many things including alcohol and, as an impressionable young man with low self-worth issues, I engaged fully.

I never learned how to put a limit or boundary on my relationship with alcohol. I got drunk every time I drank for the better part of twenty years. To clarify, my version of getting drunk always included blacking out and passing out.

Alcohol, like other substances, served a purpose for me. The purpose was not as it pertains to the integral-self but rather a purpose that served a way to hide the deep-rooted pain I was experiencing. The purpose of alcohol for me was in the realm of escape.

We can numb ourselves to current and past experiences that do not make us feel good or whole. We numb ourselves to the fact that we have unresolved issues that lead back to the early onset of childhood. Often, and more than likely, this stems from traumatic experiences. The "numbing" I describe here is always a temporary solution to a much deeper issue.

Alcohol served the purpose of numbing the sensation and feeling of unease or unhappiness, based on what I had experienced in the past. As we begin to understand how addiction works and how we can allow it to control us, we can start to recognize the patterns that truly aren't serving us, along with the ramifications that these patterns have on others. Once again, we are working in the Universal Law of Cause and Effect. Every action has a reaction or a consequence.

When we come to understand that addiction is really only a symptom we can begin to heal ourselves, however this takes time. It takes hard work and dedication to look deep within the self to understand what makes us who we are.

It's important to understand that addiction is packaged up in many different ways but we don't always realize this. It's easy, for instance, to recognize when we have an addiction to something like a narcotic or substance. It's easy to understand that someone is addicted to sex, pornography, work, projects, food, people, places and other things that don't serve them. These symptoms are simple to recognize because they provide only temporary feelings of relief. We almost always realize we are behaving in a way that is out of alignment with who we are truly destined to be. We are not standing in our own integrity when we are addicted to these experiences.

We have lost control and we have created an experience that is not serving us, yet we are unable to break free from the addiction. Why is that? The symptoms are in a different form every time, and we can "cross addict" from one addiction to another, yet the ultimate addiction lies in the behaviour and the underlying need to numb our own internal pain.

That's what I finally recognized in my own experience with addiction. I had to finally come to terms with this before I could begin to heal any further. I had to recognize that there was a constant pattern of becoming addicted to something or someone and the pattern kept recurring again and again.

I became addicted to substances that numbed me including alcohol, marijuana, magic mushrooms, LSD, ecstasy, cocaine, anti-anxiety pills and anti-depressants. I became addicted to sexual intercourse with multiple partners, finding and seeking partners without having intimate feelings towards them. I became addicted to the specific activity and lack of integrity involved with being in inappropriate relationships with women.

I even became addicted to the woman I had an affair with, the idea of her, the idea of losing her and the idea of how much pain she had caused me. I became addicted to the pain associated with losing my amazing wife and children due to the decisions that I continued to make. I became addicted to projects and work and the overall idea that the next accomplishment would be sure to satisfy me.

As a kid, you don't realize when you are addicted to food. Of all the challenges I've had in my life and the experiences I've created, my relationship with food was one of the most unrecognized addictions that contributed to my low self-worth.

For most of my childhood I was overweight. Not obese but heavier than most other children. I was a latch key kid living with a single mom and nutrition was never an important factor in our household. My mother would often leave bags of McDonald's hamburgers in the fridge as she went off to work her nursing shifts. I cannot recall any wholesome foods ever being kept in our house.

Health and wellness is still one of the greatest challenges for me to this date. I understand the reasoning behind my relationship and habits with food more than ever but I must constantly stay aware in this space. It is still not out of the question for me to have an incredible day of healthy fitness and nutrition, and then to revert to form and eat a chocolate bar at the end of the day. For many years it didn't make sense to me.

I didn't understand how this addiction to food could be so consuming. I didn't relate the soothing of emotional pain and trauma and numbing past and current experiences with food to other more prevalent addictions like drug abuse or sex abuse. Food can be an addiction too.

Many of my coaching clients have entered my program with challenges relating to relationships or severe addictions to drugs and alcohol. In most cases, they also have a food addiction and have little experience with fitness and nutrition.

Although I had many addictions and tendencies to attract similar experiences, I finally began to understand the gifts and power that these parts of me held. These gifts allowed me to recognize more power within me than I had ever experienced before. This supported a much greater healing of myself and eventually allowed me to facilitate a process to help others heal themselves.

There is caution as we move through this understanding as some forms of addiction appear to be positive and can be masks for underlying pain as well. An example is that of a workaholic. Do you find yourself immersing in project after project at work? Do you notice that often you may complete a big task or project only to be temporarily satisfied and have to start another? Do you find yourself escaping into an office environment when you could be spending time with friends and loved ones?

This is also an addiction that needs to be recognized. For years I spent my life running from one project to the next. I would aim higher and higher every time. I would seek the next award level within my company, the next title or the next financial breakthrough. I would continue to build new goals thinking that when I finally reached one of them I would be happy and satisfied.

I will speak to this further in the book, but ultimately work addiction is an addiction to two things: running away from our problems and seeking further validation from others. In either case, neither one of them is going to heal the symptoms that place limits on our highest integral-self. Of course we must continue to work, however, ideally, this new-found awareness moves us from what we call achieving to a state of receiving.

There is magic in enjoying the work or career that we have chosen. There is a major difference that exists when we become obsessed with work and use it to escape from the pain that exists within us. It is also a place of cross addiction as we may move away from what we consider unhealthy to one that society considers as success. I did this time and time again, and my obsession to my career was characterized by constantly finding time to work rather than spending time with my loved ones or working on myself.

Take a few minutes and journal in your Integrity Vow Workbook. Consider what your current work experience looks and feels like to you. Ask yourself if you have any addictive tendencies in relation to your career and if you feel that you would like to make any changes in this area. Do you find that you lose focus and the ability to stay present because you are too focused on your career?

Staying present was and continues to be a big factor in aligning with my own integral-self. I had also discovered that I was a people pleaser. Some people would indicate that anger is controlling in nature and I believe that the obsession with pleasing others works in the same way. Instead of investing in myself, I would seek to please others including the woman I was having an affair with, my wife, business partner, colleagues, family and even my children. I would try to determine what everyone else needed and try to be the problem solver for whatever issue they seemed to need help with. This too was an escape from my own pain and it did not serve me whatsoever. I eventually had to determine how I could serve myself first, before I served anyone else.

As I've mentioned, many of my clients are very successful real estate agents or business people. One of the most important discoveries that they experience when they coach with me is that they are putting everyone else before themselves.

Missing holidays, birthday parties, special moments or even time to themselves is common, and a discovery that allows them to evolve further. We focus on self-serving activity and behaviour first, before we determine how to serve and support other human beings. In my deepest truth I believe that this is of utmost importance to truly find career satisfaction.

My hope is that by now you may have begun to understand and recognize the patterns that I had personally created. Perhaps some of them resonate with your own patterns of escape or addiction. Whether it is sex, a relationship, alcohol, drugs, pornography or food, these can all show up and become addictions. They are not the *cause* of your unhappiness or despair. These are the symptoms that continue to appear in your life and as I've referenced throughout this book, they are just that: only symptoms.

They are symptoms that have differing levels of severity inside of each of us and the ramifications for each symptom will have varying effects on our quality of life. The beauty in this is that once you recognize your addictions and the underlying causes of them, you have the opportunity to immediately begin healing.

All of these symptoms have shown up to teach us about our individual challenges and allow us to begin a personal transformation. The process of healing is to move inwards and investigate our experiences that we have encountered in our lifetimes and how our current life's landscape is being created. It is in the recognition of these symptoms that we start the journey. This is a deep spiritual journey and it is an inward journey to the soul.

In doing this inner soul work, we must have courage to admit that we have addictive challenges. We must also often explore control in both areas we seek control, and areas we have lost control. Authenticity is crucial and it requires transparency, vulnerability and integrity. This is not easy work for many of us.

That's where I finally found myself on several occasions, including during the affair I had. I had been in despair for the better part of two years being sick with this addiction. I was so obsessed with her, the thought of her and the feelings attached to that thought, and even with watching her social media activities. I was constantly feeling crippling emotions such as jealousy, anger and ultimately fear. This was the addiction that I had found myself in. This was the worst that I had encountered and it was all-consuming in every area of my life. It became debilitating in every aspect and waking moment of my life. I had lost control of myself.

This was the challenge of addiction that was destroying me, and that was also destroying my family. This was the addiction that was taking me away from moments and time with my children because I was consumed in other thought. This was the addiction that prevented me from seeing the amazing parts of my wife that I had lost sight of. It was essentially bringing me to my knees and to my own rock bottom. It was the most painful addiction I had encountered and I needed help.

I tried therapy to fix it and it didn't work. I tried dissolving the relationship and it didn't work. I tried not to observe her on social media and it didn't work. I tried to create relationships to serve my ego with others and it didn't work. Nothing was working.

I was lost in the worst darkness that I had encountered in my entire life and it felt like there was no way out. I was blaming everything around me, and even though I was starting to recognize it was an addiction, I could do nothing about it at the time. I was walking around like a zombie without any focus on anyone but myself and I was completely distraught.

I was burying myself in my work projects, spending time with friends that were going through similar situations or were having their own marital challenges. When you are addicted to anything, your point of attraction is negative and can be severe and crippling. You are offering a very low vibration and working in the Universal Law of Attraction once again, where you continue to attract more of what you do not truly desire.

I would keep moving, day in and day out, not being able to sit still at home or with my kids, and I kept running away from home into other distractions.

I couldn't focus on anything my wife was trying to tell me or discuss with me while she was hurting inside, not knowing what the hell was going on in her life or with her family. How could I possibly go to work on my marriage when I was offering out such a low vibration? How could I even attempt to help my wife heal when I was still focused on the recent past?

From a physical perspective, the severity was not that of a drug addict or an alcoholic, however the emotional pain was just as debilitating. I had never been so consumed by anything in my life.

This is truly what addiction does. It shifts us to a place of minimal self-control, if any at all, if we are not aware of it. We feel like we are in control when we are soothing the addiction, but there is no possible way we are in control. We have lost the ability to make proper decisions and we continue to attach and addict to more and more non-serving thoughts and actions. We have become completely misaligned with our own integrity and highest point of attraction.

If you are addicted to anything, you have to make a choice to change. There is no way around this. You can have all the therapy, gadgets, tools or medication that are available to you, but that will not be enough. It is not always easy to share the dark parts of the self with others, and the same was true for me. My hope is that my transparency in these experiences resonates with you. When we share our story with others, it allows others to step forward with a desire to change as well.

You must realize that addiction is part of the programming that exists in all of us, and that the only way to overcome the addiction is to embrace and understand it or often it will continue or repeat itself. What I share with you is that when you do make the choice to change, and challenge the experience you are currently having that is not serving you, you will find more peace than you ever hoped for.

This is the spiritual journey that I invite you to go on if you are in any place of attachment or addiction in your life. At the beginning, it will be the most challenging journey you will ever face. You will need support from others and possibly a mentor. You will question yourself constantly and likely disagree with the process at times. It is your journey inward to make further discoveries.

If you take this place of discovery as an opportunity to learn, grow and evolve your soul, and you decide to make the journey to freedom, expansion and joy, then I assure you that you will not regret it. I assure you that there is a place beyond the pain that exists for you.

I can tell you that there are special experiences you will encounter where you will start believing in miracles and that you will be able to create your own destiny with little effort. I can tell you that the work that you will do will benefit others in your circles. You will find your freedom and you will find your bliss. You will create the version of yourself which you always knew existed deep inside of you.

You will journey to becoming whole.

If you are willing to take this journey, then I ask you to stop here and reflect for a moment. This chapter has been completely dedicated to the discoveries I made about myself in regards to addiction. Your story will be different. You may be in a place where you are having trouble physically or mentally. The spiritual path you are embarking on is one that can heal this. The question I ask is whether you feel you need healing or not.

Whatever it is that you are experiencing with addiction and attachment, I assure you there is hope. We often tell ourselves we will never resolve these experiences, but breaking free of these attachments and addictions is entirely possible. What we become addicted to is there to fill a void we have had in our souls for a long time, or perhaps even lifetimes. When you take the spiritual path to healing, you will begin to detach from these unhealthy experiences by a process of cleansing and clearing. As you begin to free yourself, you will begin to make room for the amazing things that life has to offer. You will also create the ability to manifest more and more of these experiences with ease. We will discuss detachment in the next chapter.

You are the one who is going to make choices for yourself. This is a constant process and an unwavering journey towards truth and awareness. This is the journey I invite you to take. This is the journey of the soul. I hold my hand out to you, and ask you to come on this journey with me.

Take a further vow to better understand what you may become addicted to in this lifetime. Whether it is drugs, alcohol, sexual behaviour, work, success, food or anything else, understand that the possibility exists that you may develop an addiction.

Also, understand that you have the ability to become addicted to positivity. You can create a life and experience where you constantly pursue good feelings, positive thoughts, desirable outcomes and pure happiness by stepping into your own integrity. The same driving force that may have created negative outcomes can be altered to those of a positive nature.

The choice is yours.

THE UNIVERSAL LAW OF INTENTION

We must direct energy intentionally in order to create the first step in manifesting our desires.

We direct energy with our mind and thoughts. Of course, this works together with the Law of Action which means that as we begin to get intentional, some form of action is taking place. As we discover how to direct our energy, we can begin to take action where needed in terms of our addictions and other experiences.

When it comes to the subject of addiction, I believe this is one of the most powerful laws to understand. In order to become intentional, we must have a goal or outcome in mind that we wish to achieve. In this case, I believe this would be "healing." It is important to understand here that addictions are physical elements, whereas detaching and releasing are of a spiritual nature.

As you begin to direct your energy towards healing, I believe that you will begin to see the confidence associated in doing so and understand that this intention is also one towards your integral-self. As you gain confidence and begin to make more and more positive choices, you will then become more determined to continue on this path. In essence, your intention soon becomes your reality.

As you continue to self-discover, and determine what integrity means to you, you are also in the process of healing and becoming whole. As you begin to believe that this is truly possible, you will become absolute in creating your own reality. You must believe in yourself in order to do this.

It is time to begin getting intentional with all of your thoughts and how you will step into your integrity for yourself. In order to heal, you must direct your energy towards what it is that you truly desire. Of course, the only way to do this is by taking the appropriate action steps.

Universal Law of Action

In order to create what you desire, action must be taken.

This law indicates that we must direct our energy in motion in order for manifestation to occur. This is why this law works in tandem with the Law of Intention.

Visualizing is one thing you can do, however you must understand that it is simply not enough. You must take action by actually "doing." You cannot heal yourself if you only think about what it would be like. You cannot self-discover if you do not take action and follow the appropriate steps to do so. If there is no action, then nothing will happen and there will be no result.

This is where addiction can become paralyzing. We visualize our healthier self, but we fail to take action. Even if we begin to get a little more intentional and direct our energy towards positive outcomes versus unhealthy habits, action must begin immediately.

I want to point out that there is also an addiction to self-help that exists. Self-help can be very positive in nature, however often people spend a fortune without taking serious action to get results. It is crucial to understand that reading books, going to seminars or even finding a coach are beneficial, but unless you take the appropriate amounts of *action*, your results will be limited.

There is a major difference between reading the words in a book versus studying them, internalizing them and *living* them.

For many years, I would fill up my bookshelf with the next best business or self-help books, and they would just sit there. I could also find myself reading multiple books at one time as I felt like this was an accomplishment, however I was only reading on a surface level. I don't want this to be you.

Whatever method you choose to self-discover and find your integral-self, self-discovery and spiritual work are of a deep and committed nature. If you want exceptional results, you will need to take exceptional amounts of action.

Are you prepared to take action towards a healthier you and integral-self?

Chapter 5 Exercises

Exploring any addictive challenges is the nature of this chapter and these exercises are designed for you to become more self-aware. Take the time to thoughtfully complete them and recognize what addictive challenges you may be experiencing.

1. Do you have any addictions that you are currently aware of that are not serving your highest good? Write them down in your Integrity Vow Workbook.
2. Write down the types of addictions you have had in the past. What kinds of patterns do you see with them?
3. Reflect on how these addictions have affected your life, including your physical health, relationships with loved ones and your various circumstances. Journal your discoveries in your Integrity Vow Workbook.
4. Do you feel that you need help overcoming these addictions from a place of clinical therapy or from twelve-step programs?
5. If you answered yes to #4, I want you to put down this book and make a phone call to a local twelve-step program or crisis hotline that suits the addiction in question.

CHAPTER 6

A Path of Surrender

"If you want to fly, you must give up
everything that weighs you down"

-BUDDHA

WHERE DO WE GO WHEN we are truly lost, but don't know what to do about it? Sometimes we seek answers, however waiting for these answers can feel like internal torture.

This chapter focuses on the power in surrendering and releasing ourselves from that which does not serve our integral-selves. When we detach from all of the negative thoughts, emotions, people, places and circumstances that do not truly serve us, we then release ourselves fully. This will then allow us to align with our true integral-selves where we begin to further realize that we are more powerful than ever before. This is where we stand in our own personal power. The path to surrender is not always easy, however releasing yourself from negative attachments will be one of the most liberating experiences you will ever have.

Universal Laws offer us clarity in two different ways. On one hand, we can wait patiently and the answers we are seeking will reveal themselves to us. On the other hand, we can make a swift decision and move quickly with intent in that direction. In other words, we can make a decision and then make the decision right. In my own experience, I was so attached to negative emotions associated with not only my infidelity, but with previous experiences, that I could not make any proper decisions when it came to my marriage.

Perhaps you have an ongoing circumstance that you are seeking clarity on and are having difficulty in finding answers? Whether it's a relationship or specific situation that is unclear, understanding detachment is critical to a clear mindset.

It was winter and I received a message from my wife while I was at work. She indicated that she wanted to have a discussion with me and go over some important issues at home. Things on the home front had been rocky, to say the least. We had been functioning in a state of coexistence for quite some time and we were both at a loss for answers. My mind was still wrapped up in the affair I had been carrying on for so long that I had no clue what was about to happen when I arrived home that day.

My wife had put the kids to bed for the night by the time I got there. I grabbed something to eat, took a shower and came downstairs to have our talk. I figured it would revolve around my work habits or perhaps that I wasn't pulling my weight at home. I couldn't have been more wrong.

She told me she had a few questions for me and that she had some concerns. I listened to her discuss her feelings about our marriage as she sat on the couch across the room from me. She had a stack of bills beside her and I started to think that perhaps we would be discussing financial matters. I relaxed, as this wasn't a normal matter that we would fight about and figured I could address the topic swiftly and get on with the evening.

Very quickly I realized that this was not a financial discussion. The bills that were beside her were my cellular phone bills. She wanted to bring my attention to, and ask questions about, a specific phone number that I had been calling frequently for the better part of the year. The call times lasted upwards of two to three hours on some occasions. Of course I knew the phone number that was in question, and that I was going to have to make a very quick and methodical choice. It was decision time.

In that very moment I could make one of two choices. I could lie and tell my wife any story I could think of as to why I was calling a specific out-of-town number so frequently and what the nature of the calls were. In making this choice I would be lying and once again moving away from my integral-self, but it might give me time to think and solve the problem that was being presented to me.

On the other hand, I could tell the truth and finally confess to the affair. In doing this and admitting what I had been up to for all that time I would be putting everything at risk. She could tell me to leave immediately and that she wanted a divorce. This was a reality and no one in the world would question that decision or blame her for making it. This was a monumental moment in the course of our marriage.

I surrendered.

As the tears rolled down my face I explained my infidelity in full detail. I explained how it started, why I felt it started, and the details of my affair. I explained that I was incredibly sorry for any hurt I had caused and that I understood if she no longer wanted to be married. I explained how sick I had allowed the affair to make me, and that I was not in integrity at all. I explained that I was seeking help to become a better human being.

Over the next couple of weeks I embarrassingly told my wife every single gruesome detail about the affair and the woman I had been with. My wife had no intention of confronting the other woman, but she simply wanted to understand the reasons why it happened. It was an absolutely painful experience to expose those details to someone who has been completely genuine and truthful the entire time I have known her.

I've worked with and continue to work with many coaching clients who face moments of truth such as this one. These are moments where our integrity is front and centre and we get to make a choice to step into our own power or not.

In my own relationship with my wife, I also explained that as a result of my poor choices, and my awareness that I was not well, I had begun to seek additional guidance. I was going to do some coaching with someone who had experience with unhealthy patterns. I told my wife that although I was hoping it would improve our marriage, I felt as though I needed this help for myself first, and that it would then transfer over to our children and her.

What I hadn't realized at the time was that I was already on a path of surrendering and releasing all of the negative circumstances that were surrounding me and inside of me. I hope that you realize you are doing the same in reading this book. When we determine that we cannot fix everything for ourselves, and we begin to seek guidance and help from others, we are releasing ourselves from the expectation of needing to know how to figure it all out. This is a very freeing and uplifting experience that you will continue to have as you begin to surrender your own attachments.

In the two weeks when I admitted all the nasty details of the affair I found something I could not recall experiencing before. I was detached from the outcomes associated with not only the affair, but my marriage as well. I understood that my marriage was possibly going to end. I understood that the relationship with my children might be greatly affected. I understood that my friends, family and colleagues may have a different opinion of who I was as a father and man. I detached from all of it and it was one of the most relieving experiences of my life.

The most amazing part of this experience was that it encapsulated all of my previous experiences. It was a moment of realization that I had been attached to so many negative aspects my entire life. As I began to let go of the negative emotions such as shame, jealousy, guilt, anger, resentment, sadness and all of the parts of me that created low self-worth, I began to free myself. I reflected on many of my addictive traits as well with alcohol, drug abuse, sex, violence and even workaholism and began to realize the freedom in releasing these too. I started to feel lighter and lighter as I discovered more. I am sure you will continue to experience much of the same.

I'll shed more light on my wife later in this book, but what I share with you is that I have never once met someone with so much strength and dignity in my life. To say that she handled the news, pain and struggle that this caused with the utmost integrity is an understatement.

Her strength was admirable, and so I began to go to work on myself. This was a journey to the soul, and I had to learn more about myself in order to heal. I also began considering if I had it in me to repair my marriage and actually go to work on it. I was not out of the woods though and there was much to do when it came to understanding who I was. In order to heal my marriage in any way, I would need to heal myself.

Even though I was discovering my integral-self, I was still a completely mixed bag of emotions. My primary focus was to create a healthier version of myself by understanding what had caused the current experience that I was having. I also wanted to ensure it didn't happen again.

What an emotional roller coaster, filled with varying emotions such as guilt, shame, anger, jealousy, sadness, relief, hope, happiness and peace. The challenge was that it was a back and forth struggle to find the positive emotions associated with my progress, versus reverting to form and attaching to the negative ones.

I don't think anyone in the world, including my wife and children, wanted to be around me at that time even though I was allowed to remain living in the house. I still remember my oldest son telling my wife he wished I would leave our home after he observed my wife and I having an argument. What a heart breaking experience to hear those words from one of your children.

My staff at work could see glimpses of leadership one day and a rattled shell of a man the next. Why were all of these emotions swirling around inside of me? Why were the negative emotions being allowed to impact my family and friends to the degree that they were? What was it inside of me that was crying for more of the happiness and freedom I had begun to discover but couldn't quite fully tune into?

I had learned by then that it is possible to choose your feelings or direct your energy to positive thoughts, but something was getting in the way of me actually doing so. Finding the solution in this would be a challenging journey, taking me further down the spiritual path.

I began to reflect on the affair, as I was not fully clear of the emotional attachments associated with it. I recalled all the times where temporary excitement in the moment was followed by long periods of guilt and shame. This, of course, had much to do with the attachment style that originated in my childhood.

This is a good time to pause and examine your own experience based on the reading so far. Have you begun to do more self-reflection and examine your authentic self? Have you explored addiction and attachment fully and do you realize what's created some of your current circumstances? Are you prepared to surrender to your own integrity? Journal your answers in the Integrity Vow Workbook.

As I look back now, I realize I did not enjoy much of my infidelity. I would always be rushing home late and stopping by my office or a public restroom as I needed to brush my teeth, wash my face, put deodorant on and hide any smells or evidence. If that isn't enough to indicate to someone that what they are doing isn't the right thing to be doing, I don't know what is.

Those are the moments and times when you feel ashamed of your behaviour. The moments when you are all alone and you are hiding something from someone else who really doesn't deserve to have anything hidden from them. These are moments where we act out of integrity, often without realizing why we are doing so.

As I reflected I began to feel more and more guilt and shame. Somehow I would need to detach from these emotions as well. Of course we all have regrets in life, but holding onto them in a lower vibration when it comes to energy and attracting more of that energy will not allow good experiences to unfold, doing no one any kind of good.

There is a reason that an addict remains attached to an addiction such as this one. There are emotions that we do not recognize as we enter into this type of relationship. Often we are only looking for the instant gratification that we believe it will bring us. Many times we do not realize that our past experiences have programmed us to seek more of these experiences. It is such an unhealthy cycle and I highly encourage you to do a deep study to gain further understanding of your own attachment style.

As you surrender further, you are going to realize that your current experience correlates with so many others. Whether it was cocaine, projects, relationships or even an attachment to the fear of being successful, they all shared the same underlying premise for me. I was attached to experiences that created the feelings and notion of low self-worth.

What starts off innocent or passionate turns to jealousy, shame, anger and a whole other series of trust issues that we likely hadn't discovered about ourselves. This was certainly the case in my own experience. Often we don't realize that these emotions can have such an unhealthy impact on our lives and the lives of others. Often times it's hard to understand how the current experience has allowed us to become so emotionally unstable. What we often may not realize is that we've encountered this instability before.

Humans can become completely attached to a thought or person and the ramifications can be severe. The damage that we do to ourselves by moving out of integrity, living in a state of fear at times and remaining attached to this experience can be detrimental to our health. You may have experienced the physical ramifications of unhealthy attachments yourself. Attaching at this level can also manifest illness. As we continue to resist the healthy and integral-self, we often create energy blockages which can turn into physical ailments.

Affairs are rarely relationships that end well. The lack of trust, integrity and self-worth that accompany this kind of relationship does not typically support a high success rate when it comes to a long lasting, loving experience. I realize that some exceptions do exist, however from my perspective an affair is a very outcome-based attachment. Further, as we come to understand internal versus external outcomes, infidelity does not often support personal integrity. When we are cheating on others, we are also cheating on ourselves. Have you ever felt like you are cheating yourself out of true integrity-based happiness?

If you are in the middle of an affair, or perhaps contemplating stepping out of your integrity to enter an inappropriate relationship, I believe this book will support you in reconsidering that choice. Only you can make your own specific choices, however pausing to consider your actions and possible consequences is a healthy habit to get into.

I clarify here that the premise of this book is not just about infidelity. Many of my coaching clients are experiencing the exact same feelings as they pertain to different areas of their lives. The common theme is an attachment to lower vibrational thoughts and activities.

One of my favourite coaching clients is incredibly successful in business. He earns over one million dollars in real estate commissions each and every year and began coaching with me to create more quality of life inside of his business. As he began to self-discover, he started to reference the relationship he'd had with his mother when he was a child. She had created a great divide in the family dynamic and was absent much of the time.

My client was very resentful of his mother. He realized that he was trying to please her to create his own self-worth during his entire life, right up until the day that his mother passed away. He began to recognize that this realization of pleasing also pertained to many of the relationships he had with his own children, wife and even clients. The work that we did together allowed him to understand his own attachment style and how it impacted every relationship he was involved in.

When he began to create boundaries, his time and quality of life began to increase, however this brought on the discovery of another negative attachment he was experiencing, which was an attachment to the powerful and often debilitating emotion of anger.

As he began to understand how anger is a fear-based emotion and to realize it would not serve him to continue to stay angry with his mother or himself, he began to experience freedom. The more and more he released this anger, the more and more freedom and happiness he experienced. He did this when he surrendered.

It doesn't matter whether you are in an unhealthy relationship or not. It doesn't matter if you are addicted to a person, place or thing. You can always make changes if you have a desire to do so. In my deepest truth and as it applied to my own experience, relationships can be healed if we work on healing the self. This is a very integral-based choice that we must consider as individuals, based on what feels right in each unique experience. It requires constant reflection and self-exploration, which is also a choice you must make for spiritual growth.

I believe our astounding divorce rate in today's society has much to do with the fact that we do not understand ourselves as we need to, before we enter into a commitment that marriage entails. It was true in my own experience and holds true for the vast majority of my coaching clients that experience challenges in their relationships. We must continue to release ourselves from negative attachments in order to free up the positivity that can unfold in a harmonious relationship with someone else. It can be done.

You see, we humans have the ability to get so lost that it appears to become easier to accept failure instead of success sometimes. Depending on each individual circumstance, we must understand that even failures are opportunities. I will tell you and I'll show you that I got pretty much as deep into a marital mess as anyone could. With the proper process and commitment to doing the work, I was able to remove myself from that darkness, to reclaim my own personal power and to repair a great deal of damage I had done in my marriage and to my family.

It takes time, relentless dedication, a little hope, and hopefully someone is still willing to see your effort. My wife was absolutely exceptional through the process and I am forever grateful to her.

There have been challenging moments, of course. You don't just walk into an inappropriate relationship like that and you certainly don't just walk out of it either. The same goes for a marriage that is facing challenges or suffering. There are emotions and feelings that require time and healing. What I share is that as you begin to self-discover and learn more of the integral and creative process for yourself, you will be able to choose much more positive emotions that will serve you in healing outer circumstances.

This is a very rewarding gift to give yourself. How much more would you enjoy life if you didn't get consumed in thought or if you were not attached to the experiences that don't serve you at the highest level?

Attachment to thought can consume every second and every minute of our time if we are not careful. It prevents us from concentrating on other more meaningful relationships, work, school or whatever we are supposed to be mindful of in the moment. It literally puts us in an unhealthy trance that is fuelled by fear, and ultimately many emotions pertaining to low self-worth.

Even after I told my wife about the affair and ceased contact with the woman I had been seeing, I continued to observe and watch her from a distance. I had even blocked her on my phones and removed her from my social media contacts. For some reason I continued to watch though, as I was still attached to some of the specific emotions associated with her. I was primarily experiencing jealousy, which is a very fear-based emotion that is attached to outcomes and fuelled with anger. This may seem unfair and I wish that I could have tuned into a more positive emotion towards my marriage at the time, however I had not equipped myself with the proper navigational or coping skills quite yet.

What I came to understand was that I wasn't really jealous about another person. I was really only trying to learn about and understand myself further. I had an attachment style that originated from the relationship with my mother as my primary caregiver. This early attachment style was something I would need to explore and surrender to in order to free myself. It took me a long time to understand that the fear of being powerless was what drove the obsession, as these were experiences I had faced throughout my entire lifetime.

I understand if the thought process doesn't make sense to you as you read this. It didn't make sense to me either, however this is the result of attachment. We become consumed and focused on nothing but our attachments without having a conscious understanding of why.

An attachment to any negative emotion prevents us from making responsible decisions. If we are addicts, and I was, we become focused on the one and only thing we want and cannot see with a clear perspective. We don't realize that the danger and decisions we are making will have a profound ripple effect in every other area of our lives. We are attached to a thought, and it becomes compulsive.

We humans have a wonderful way of seeking to control everything that exists outside of us. We believe that our actions will alter the normal flow of the universe at times, which simply isn't so. What I share with you is that you do have an amazing gift of power, but it ultimately lies within you rather than outside of you. As I began to discover what my own integral-self looked like, I began to understand this much more clearly.

I began to realize that every single thing I needed in my life ultimately lay within. I had to learn how to serve myself at a higher level before I could serve my family at a higher level. I could not do this until I started to release the negative aspects of myself first.

It wasn't the affair that was the challenge with the experience I had created with my family. It was the addiction and attachment to all the experiences of drama and chaos that had been created my entire life. Each time I tried to reproduce self-worth by trying to control or manipulate my external world, the pattern of drama and chaos continued. It was as if I could package it all up in a box and send it to myself in the mail. I never liked what came in the delivery, so I would send it back and repackage it with different wrapping. The experience continued time and time again until I learned to release myself.

My entire childhood consisted of trauma, abuse, experiences of low self-worth and fear. This had created many emotions such as anger, jealousy, and sadness that I was attached to. This was my point of attraction and the programming that existed within me that sought out to attract more of the same. We will look at this further, and how you can identify your own point of attraction, later in this book.

For most of my childhood I experienced chaos and hostility. Thus, many of the relationships I was involved with included much of the same before I met my wife. For addicts, it is often times challenging to feel, and we seek out circumstances in order to feel what we think we are supposed to. In most cases we think that this is love, however often we don't realize what love truly is in these situations.

As I began to learn more about the powerful Universal Laws I started to increase my own awareness. This was a very powerful experience as awareness is a crucial aspect of understanding anything at a deep level. The only way I could do this was to surrender and release the negative. I could not experience a heightened state of awareness or higher experience of consciousness without cleansing and clearing myself through a path of surrendering.

Envision all of the aspects of your life as glasses that are overfilling with everything that you have encountered so far in your lifetime. One of your glasses may be your family. Another glass may be your career. Perhaps another would be your relationship with your spouse or children. What I want you to do is picture yourself emptying each glass half way. When you empty the glass, you only keep the positive parts of yourself and let the other parts go down the drain. You now have a glass that's half full with the most amazing parts of you and your life. You also have room for so much more if you allow yourself to experience them.

As you begin to come to terms with what you may be attached to in your own experience, I believe your heightened sense of awareness will serve you like never before. Perhaps you have people or thoughts that you know you would like to release yourself from. Perhaps you have circumstances you feel you cannot break free from, or perhaps you don't know how to overcome certain obstacles. Perhaps you are attached to a fantasy or relationship that is out of integrity and you do not realize why.

As you continue on with this reading, you will begin to learn more of the self-discovery process and identify what your own path of integrity looks like. You will develop rituals, habits and an increased sense of awareness and self-worth that will allow you to move into better experiences all around.

In the meantime, let's visit the subject of this chapter and how Universal Laws directly impact release and detachment.

UNIVERSAL LAW OF DETACHMENT

This is the law that allows us to release what we feel it is that we desire. It is a law that is among the most challenging to utilize, however it can be one of the most freeing experiences and can allow the other Universal Laws to work with ease.

It is important to understand the outcome that you truly desire, however a certain level of detachment must occur in order to work with your integral-self and the manifestation process.

In other words, attach to the process of manifestation and *detach* from the outcome associated with it. This law works with the Universal Law of Allowing.

As you begin to understand energy and the power of your emotions, especially when combined with the Universal Laws, detachment will allow you to remove the negative emotional charges that pertain to certain situations or experiences.

Remember that your thoughts create your reality and that it is important to revisit the Law of Vibration in every experience we wish to create. Depending on how your thoughts are charged, this works too with all of the other Universal Laws.

When you create a positive thought, your outcome will be much more desirable than when you charge a thought with a negative emotion. It is important to understand how these negative emotions originated and begin to surrender, release and detach from all of them. As you embark on this process you will continue to raise your vibration with more ease. Remember that this is your point of attraction.

I want you to begin to investigate your thoughts and understand that when you are charging your thoughts with fear, jealousy, anger and worry, you are attached to an outcome. Where did this originate? What is your own attachment style and what must you release?

This goes back to the programming and experiences we have encountered throughout our entire lifetimes. Perhaps there were experiences where you were told that you were not good enough, or you endured loss and abandonment leading to lower self-worth. What we seek is to find answers in this discovery to understand ourselves further, and to cleanse the negative emotions attached to these experiences. The unconscious mind can be wicked, and often we do not even realize we are attached to these thoughts.

My purpose is to assist you in steering clear of some of these negative emotions that can render you powerless, moving outside of your integral-self. These would include:

* Melancholy
* Hostility or Anger
* Heartbreak
* Scarcity

If you are holding any negative emotion and attaching it to that which you desire, you will not create it as the Law of Attraction does not work this way. Remember...like attracts like. Thus, you will likely attract the very opposite of what you're intending.

I want you to come to understand you no longer have to accept a negative outcome as a possibility. The best way to do this is to detach from not only the negative emotion associated with an outcome, but the outcome itself. Instead, I want you to begin to feel the positive emotion associated with that which you wish to create.

There's a great exercise that will give you a sense of this in your own state of awareness. Make a fist as tight as you possibly can to the point where you can't clench any further. Consider the stress that this fist holds, and hold it for thirty seconds. By the time you hit thirty seconds, you will be feeling the sense of exhaustion, even in your hand. Now release your fist and feel the immediate sense of freedom as you let go of all the exhausting energy that existed in your clenched fist.

Revisit the principles we've discussed earlier in this book and study them. Understand your point of attraction and what vibration you may be offering to the Universe at any given moment. Are you a negative magnet or a positive magnet?

What outcomes are you still trying to control with the negative emotions that you may have attached to? Let go of anything that hinders your spiritual growth, whether it's a toxic emotion or a toxic relationship, and you will begin to allow the powerful Universal Laws to work freely and flow through you like never before.

I want you to become so intentional about understanding your emotions and how you direct your energy that nothing but goodness will come your way. We will continue to work on the process of doing so in order to create every positive outcome that you desire.

My hope for you is that you make a clear and concise decision to detach and remove yourself from any person, place or thing that does not serve you. I am sure you will understand with compassion and empathy that everyone is on his or her own journey and that sometimes our paths were meant to cross for a reason, however it does not always mean that we will continue on that journey with them.

Release yourself from the experience of trying to control the behaviour of other people. Release yourself from expectations that don't really serve you. Release yourself from the attachments that you have created and that have been buried deep within for many years. Release yourself from toxic or negative emotions.

In doing this you will find more of the happiness and freedom that you desire and deserve. You will find your integrity, the self-worth and pride inside of that discovery. Surrendering to your truths will end up being easier than ever before.

You will also begin to live with grace.

CHAPTER 6 EXERCISES

When you open yourself to detachment and surrender, you will experience great discoveries. These exercises will aid you in that, and allow you to explore where you must next go on your path.

1. What people, places and circumstances are you currently consumed with? Journal your answers.
2. Consider in what areas of your own individual experience you could surrender. Journal your answers.
3. If you could think of one word to describe your "attachments," what would it be?
4. What is it you have not released that no longer serves you? Journal your answers in your Integrity Vow Workbook.

CHAPTER 7
Truth and Transparency

"Peace is the beauty of life. It is sunshine. It is the smile
of a child, the love of a mother, the joy of a father, the
togetherness of a family. It is the advancement of man,
the victory of a just cause, the triumph of truth"

-MENACHEM BEGIN

SOME SAY THAT THE TRUTH will set you free. Others say that our
sickness is in our secrets. I had finally told the truth at home and
begun the process of clearing the secrets that remained within me.

This chapter places an emphasis on the importance of discovering our own truths. We will also focus on the importance of bringing our truth forward working in the Law of Authenticity, which
requires vulnerability, integrity and transparency. As you continue
to discover your integral-self, you will increase your awareness to
your own personal truths.

By normal societal standards I looked like I had a lot to be proud
of in my life. I had a family which included a beautiful wife and three
incredible sons. I had several different careers that brought forth
financial success. I had a nice house and a nice car. I had received
recognition countless times from my industry and created a thriving
real estate company. Anyone would think I had a lot to be proud of.

Similarly, many of my coaching clients have experienced what others also consider "success." Unfortunately this success is often on a surface level and covers deep and dark secrets that often surface in our work together.

The truth was, I was miserable. I wasn't proud of any of my business accomplishments. I appreciated my wife and adored my children, however I wasn't proud of myself as a husband or father. It didn't matter what family photo you pulled out during those years, whatever smile I had on my face was fake.

I'm not saying I didn't take joy in experiencing those moments with my family. What I'm saying is that behind the smile and the family man image I was experiencing a lot of pain that nobody really knew about. Until I made the choice to discover the truth about myself, I didn't understand the pain I was going through.

In essence, I was showing up each day in a variety of different roles that I felt defined me. These roles consisted of the business man, daddy, husband, soccer coach, hockey trainer, parent association rep and so on. All of these roles were supposed to bring me a sense of satisfaction and pride, however, they did not.

It was somewhat confusing as I didn't realize what I actually wanted, and was confused about what was really happening at home. I was just getting by, going along in each role, because that's what society had me thinking I needed to do in order to be happy. What an illusion that was.

Take a moment and journal what roles you play in your own life. In your Integrity Vow Workbook, write down the different roles, and whether or not they feel authentic to you. This can be a challenging exercise but one that gives great reflection on your own integral-self. When I first starting recognizing my own roles, I realized I had many of them that did not align with my own integrity.

It really didn't matter what any of them were, and I realized I had a long process of self-discovery ahead of me. I had to walk backwards through the chapters of my life analyzing and investigating everything I had experienced and what shaped the outcomes I was currently living. I had done some pretty great things with family and my career, but I needed to understand why I couldn't feel good about them. I wanted to learn about pride and what true satisfaction actually felt like.

I began by looking at the experience I had created as a result of my infidelity. This included examining the challenges and devastation that it was causing inside of my marriage and with the relationship that I hoped to have with my children and wife. I considered how this experience made me feel about myself.

There was truth to discover in the work that I was doing inside of my career, and I came to understand that it was a constant escape into each new project, trying to find solitude from a life that I was running from.

It was also important to consider all of the years of alcohol and drug abuse by reliving many of those experiences all the way back to when I took my first drink, first smoke and first line of cocaine.

There was the memory of losing my childhood friend who was someone I considered to be a benchmark for what love looked like. I allowed myself to finally feel what that pain was and what it showed up to teach me.

I walked backwards further, to the bullying I encountered in elementary school and the lack of self-worth those experiences had created at an early age.

In fact, it was a process where I began to study all of the effects my early childhood had had on me, including physical and emotional abuse. I had to come to terms with the experience of abandonment and, although I didn't blame my parents for this, with the impact that these events had on my life and the early programming I had endured that had shaped much of my existence.

This also included exploring my own attachment style. The early childhood years often create levels of attachment that impact all of our future relationships. This would provide great insight into the way that I communicated and my emotional response to many of the people, places and circumstances I encountered.

If you follow the Law of Attraction, you understand that we attract what we are, not what we want. Every circumstance that I had lived up until that point was a complete manifestation of the experiences I had created. Understanding the truth about personal responsibility and choice were crucial in the beginning of my transformation.

There was a pattern of attracting people, places and things for the better part of over thirty years that did not serve my higher purpose. I attracted the addicts, the workaholics, the bullies, the liars, the thieves, the abandoners, the dishonest, the cruel, the lost, the dark and the forgotten.

All of these manifestations were not what I wanted, as nobody would consciously want those things. The truth in this discovery was that all of those traits existed in me. This can be a challenging principle to understand and pertains to the Universal Law of One or Oneness which I encourage you to explore further.

In my own self-discovery, I was beginning to understand that I needed to work in purpose rather than trying to hide my true integral-self. The transformation I originally began was of a manipulative nature in which I was trying to convince others of my worth. As I've referenced earlier, the truth is that validation only exists within. This was a hard principle for me to grasp in my own experience, but one that is so very liberating.

I was also manipulating my own integrity by creating change for the wrong reasons. I wanted to show everyone that I felt had ever wronged me, bullied me, cheated on me or even abandoned me that I was worthy of much more. Ultimately, this form of gratification was only temporary and I needed to shift my perspective here as well.

Everything I had been doing was a desire to control external circumstances. It was seeking to find power from the outside world. I was not happy or healed inside my own experience so I was seeking to abuse substances, work projects and people to gain power. The Universe does not work this way. I could no longer hide in my outside world, rather I would need to discover the truth about my inside world.

When we try to control others by creating experiences that breed envy, jealousy, anger or even sadness, we are still seeking validation from the outside world. This too is a form of fear-based action. It is a fear of what others may think and a fear of how others may react. When we work in the emotion of anger, we come to realize that we still have a spiritual fracture that requires resolution.

It is with the lens that we see life through that we get to determine for ourselves the amount of joy we experience. This goes for people, places and things and all of the experiences that we create. Ultimately there comes a point in time where we must come to a decision for ourselves whether the experiences and things that are showing up are joyous or not.

Again, this revolves around the power of choice. It also requires the vulnerability to allow ourselves to step forward with transparency, regardless of what others may think.

There is hope for you in uncovering your own truths and what they mean to you. The more transparent that you are in regards to your own integral-self, the more you will continue to evolve and grow your spiritual-self.

I've had several coaching clients who discovered that their career choices were not serving their higher selves. When they came to understand the truth, and bring forward the fear of leaving a stable career, they were able to determine what choices they could then make to grow and evolve further. These clients have all made decisions to find more fulfilling careers, and despite the uncertainty at the time, they are now completely satisfied with their decisions and enjoying more fulfilling paths.

You may also find that this principle resonates when it comes to relationships. Whether you've been betrayed, have been involved inappropriately or have had other challenges inside of the relationship with yourself, determining your own truth is crucial.

I have discovered that all of my readers and coaching clients are similar to me in that they eventually realize this at some point in time. It is not the objects we seek that bring us the joy we desire.

Instead it is the feelings we think we'll experience once we get the object. What things and circumstances do you desire? What about them do you feel would bring you joy? Journal your answers in your Integrity Vow Workbook.

What a daunting truth to face, in that I was finding replacements for love, health, freedom or joy, but I was not embracing them as they were not in alignment with my integral-self. I was finding outside experiences and things to create an illusion about what I was experiencing.

So the truth began to set me free. Many experts or theorists indicate that there is a point in time a human being must go through to get to this place. This is the experience that will ultimately take us to a decision process of not only wanting to make changes in our lives, but of having an inner knowing about those changes. Unless we make the changes, we will remain troubled and in despair. When we determine what our own truths are, we step into our own integrity and then allow for the experiences we desire to come to fruition.

I had been living in inner turmoil for so long in my marriage that I wasn't truly sure of what I wanted. I didn't know what the truth was when it came to the desired outcome for my wife and me. It was a vicious cycle and I could feel myself dying inside. I even went to a psychic to try and find guidance. The psychic told me that whatever I decided, I would be making the right decision, but I could not stay in this place of unease or confusion or I would actually become physically ill.

I cannot say for certain, but I believe she saw the resistance I had created in understanding my own truth, and she envisioned illness in my future. Remember that the Universal Law of Resistance indicates that when we resist certain aspects of ourselves, we create negative blockages of energy that can manifest in physical illness. Thankfully, years later, she believes I will live a long life.

Although I had left my marriage both physically and spiritually for a period of time, I also knew that I had returned home and I needed to understand why I made this decision. I had been to see a therapist for about six months at this point as I just wasn't functioning well trying to figure it all out. I was so wrapped up in my headspace that it appeared I couldn't feel my way through anything.

Although my therapist had told me that only I could make an integral decision about the outcome of my marriage, there were many times I wanted to grab onto my wife and ask her to save me. I wanted to tell her I was lost and confused and longed for a place of peace between us. I had spent so many years trying to cope and control all of the external circumstances around me that I never addressed this with her. The truth of the matter was I knew how secure she made me feel. This felt good to me.

It's a vulnerable position we find ourselves in when we address our challenges, struggles or concerns with someone. It requires a very authentic and transparent choice to bring this to the attention of others. In my own experience, and with any of my coaching clients, I am certain that the more transparent we are, the better results we find.

I decided to keep telling her the truth about anything that she wanted to ask me. She wanted full transparency and I gave her that because she deserved it. I don't think I have more respect for another human being than my wife, for the way that she handled the information that I shared with her. I don't believe I've met a stronger woman in my entire life, one who would have handled that information and knowledge about her husband with so much grace.

She could have left or pushed me away, and I often wonder how she found the courage to stay. She is the strongest human being I have encountered and I am grateful to have met her in my lifetime.

She is a warrior.

Looking into my wife's eyes and seeing the pain I had caused can never be erased. You get to understand the Law of Cause and Effect quite clearly in these circumstances. Every choice has an outcome or consequence and I was living that consequence in my reality.

What was freeing about disclosing this truth was that she also took some responsibility for our marital breakdown. I didn't expect her to at the time as I had created so much of the experience, but she did anyway. That made a major difference in our marriage and led us to at least keep trying. We both explained some of our truths, which also allowed us to understand ourselves better.

In my own situation, this still presented some challenges. It shouldn't have been difficult if we had a clean slate, however I admit that it was. It wasn't the norm for me to be standing and living in truth and transparency.

I had spent so long placing control on my privacy and forms of communication that it was going to be hard to release that control. I wanted my wife to see that I was honest and not a complete liar all the time, and that I really wanted to change. I wanted to be there for her for the first time in a long time as I could see the pain I had caused her, but I could also see her protection of our family. I don't believe that I gave her enough time to express herself fully, however the transparency I did give allowed our marriage to continue.

A relationship will not survive without trust. Not even close, if you want it to be healthy and harmonious. It is crucial in any situation, whether it's a marriage, a business relationship or the parent-child bond, that we must be absolutely transparent when trust is lost.

You will also discover that the more transparent you are, the more you will be able to work on yourself with ease. It was a lot of work being me for many years if you know what I mean. Truth and transparency ends all that, regardless of what the outcome is. This is the time to set yourself free and trust in the Universe.

All people have their own stories and their own challenges to face in life, but I had never found a productive way to deal with mine. I did not know how to resolve conflict, which I had a great deal of in my childhood. I did not know how to deal with the initial parts of abandonment that I faced as a child, which were matters that were out of my control. In fact all of the beliefs and ideas that were formulated in my childhood created some severe barriers to growth. There was a lot of programming from those early years that prevented me from seeing the truth about my experiences.

Sometimes the hardest part of growing spiritually is to face our own truth rather than accepting the opinions or standards that society places upon us. This can even pertain to a professional diagnosis.

When I decided to seek out a therapist to determine what made me try to control everything in my life or create a better version of myself, I had good intentions of doing so. We worked together for about six months and although she had some good insight, I was just going through the motions. The clinical approach wasn't working for me. I also found this to be true later on, when I worked with a relationship therapist with my wife.

I felt like she was trying to compartmentalize the trauma I had experienced as a young child and to determine how to delete this from what she called the "little black box" inside of my head. I think the challenge I have with traditional therapists is that they really focus on what's wrong with you. There was very little focus on what was working for me, what was right. I speak a lot on deliberate creation and the Law of Attraction, and holding onto these negative thoughts in a room for an hour wasn't serving me very well.

I believe that much of what I was learning was holding me in a negative vibrational thought pattern. I have now come to recognize that finding the highest vibration possible is what serves my clients and I at a higher level.

On the other hand, my coach and personal development mentor was taking a different approach. He knew that I was in an inappropriate relationship. He understood the programming I had encountered as a child and some of the other experiences I had created. We touched on it and looked at the cause behind it, but we quickly moved in a different direction. Much of this coaching revolved around health and fitness instead.

I asked him about his own traumatic experiences and how he had eliminated them and he told me that he hadn't. He had been a severe alcoholic before his own transformation began and he didn't try to delete those experiences from his little black box. Instead, he embraced some of this darkness and allowed it to remain in his experience and shape future experiences in a positive way. He referred to this as standing in his own truth.

I decided to do what I called a 90-Day Cleanse, which I created for myself. I was going to go ninety days clean and clear of anything toxic. My coach facilitated an idea exchange for fitness and nutrition while I decided on other experiences I needed to move my attention away from. These were the truthful and toxic experiences that I had created and they included people, places and things. So I began.

It was interesting to get started with this. It gave me something to do in the mornings when I created a routine of getting up and working out. I didn't do the nutrition very well in the first ninety days, but I stopped drinking alcohol for that time. I wasn't going to stop forever, but I figured it would be a good test.

I even created a couple of social media pages to track my progress and results. I found that the more transparent I was with others, the more I committed to the work I was doing. I also believe that public declaration results in quicker manifestation. Sharing my story became a regular part of my day.

I noticed some differences fairly quickly. My energy level increase was the most dramatic difference as suddenly I wasn't hung over and my bouts of depression were few and far between. This allowed me to raise my vibration and offer better energy in my day-to-day life.

As I detached from the negative and toxic parts of my life, I began to experience a great deal of different emotions. My most recent experience was the affair, and I had lingering feelings of anger, jealousy, resentment and guilt. What I came to understand as I sat in my own truth was that these were all consequences of the choices that I had made. I didn't blame the other woman anymore for her role in the experience. I owned it and understood that it was I alone who would choose to feel this way.

This completely changed the way I thought about all of my experiences relating to my infidelity. Everything I had been doing and feeling was a direct result of the original choice that I made to be with her. I hadn't taken any responsibility for that and it allowed me to start focusing solely on the choices I had made. I realized these were my own issues rather than blaming someone else for the circumstances that surrounded me. Ultimately what it was doing was giving me my own power back, because I wasn't releasing that to someone else or trying to control someone else's outcome. The truth is that if we want power, we must give up control.

There was great satisfaction I took in discovering the power within me and the truth in how that shaped me. I started to notice significant changes both physically and emotionally. My body began to change as I had literally quit drinking and was without a drop of alcohol for ninety days. I was working out more than I ever had as I found it therapeutic. I was beginning to lose weight and have my body feel good. My energy at home in the mornings without being hung over was a major improvement compared to what I had been doing for years and years.

Missing alcohol wasn't a big deal either. Sure there were times that I would be with friends and want to share in a drink, but I had committed to the ninety days and wanted to see it through. Alcohol is a definite depressant, so to be able to eliminate parts of that allowed me to feel better about myself. It was a crucial step with my wife as well. All those moments that I had destroyed over the years due to my drinking had taken a toll on her and my children.

She began to recognize some of my work efforts towards changing, which I believe gave her hope that she hadn't felt in at least a decade. We were nowhere close to being "fixed" from a marital standpoint, but the fact that her alcohol abusing husband was limiting his drinking must have given her a sign that he may be able to make some other changes too. Perhaps we may have attached too much to that outcome, but it was a start in healing to some degree.

My kids started to get on board with it as well. They liked that my body was changing and they noticed that their mother and I weren't fighting as much. It was a simple place of personal choices and responsibility for ninety days that seemed to help me make some changes. I had begun to understand the truth about my relationship with alcohol and how it impacted my overall well-being.

Many of my coaching clients discover much of the same when they embark on their own personal growth. One of my clients who comes to mind was having major self-worth challenges and had considered suicide at one point. As he started to work on his body with a proven fitness and nutrition plan, he began to build up his own self-worth. As he shared his story of progress on social media, he had a tremendous response which allowed others to step forward and share their own story. The satisfaction he received in helping others was unparalleled with anything he had experienced before. He began to truly understand what his purpose was.

After I had taken a break from my therapist, I returned as I had some paid sessions left. When I came back my therapist even noticed I had dropped some weight and my energy had transformed. It was a strange experience though. There was very little discussion on the positive changes I was making and more discussion on the unresolved issues from my childhood. She wanted to investigate the black box further and move away from me focusing on my health and fitness so much, as she felt that this was another form of addiction.

Of course there is the clinical approach to this in that I could be cross addicting into something else, even if the project was my health. I didn't care for her approach though, as it just didn't feel good. I understood that I needed to focus on the various parts of me that existed deep inside, but I felt her method had a negative vibration to it. Leaving her office always created a lower point of attraction than the good feelings associated with leaving the gym. This too was my own recognition of truth.

I had never felt as good inside because of the changes I was making to my body. My therapist told me that she wanted me to take my focus off of my physical transformation and put the focus into what I really needed to work on. Whether she was right or wrong, whether I was right or wrong, this approach was not going to work for me. I thanked her for her time, told her to keep the thousand dollars for pre-paid sessions with her, and got up and walked out of her office.

Everybody has a different way of doing things. Nobody was going to control how I felt any longer, as I had begun to feel good about myself for what may have been the first time in my life. I wanted to stay in my own personal place of self-empowerment. I must reference that many of my clients, friends and family have had exceptional results with clinical therapists, however this model and that particular therapist were not assisting me in where I needed to go and what I wanted to create.

My physical transformation also began to lead to other things. People suddenly started noticing a difference and were very encouraging along with curious about what I was doing. In my own truth, I needed to stay very aware in this space because there is a strong validation aspect that is created when people recognize physical changes. At the beginning of my transformation I admit that there was still a part of me that was seeking validation from others.

I was trying to prove to anyone that ever picked on me or bullied me that I was going to be different than any way they had ever experienced me before. The challenge in this was that it was the same old story that I was creating once again.

I was in a new project, which was trying to prove something to others. It was completely a showcase to try and control what others thought of me. It was a continuation of unhealthy thinking. It also wasn't the right thinking to naturally ease into the process of correcting and improving the relationship I had with my wife and children. I had to go further inward and understand more of my truths.

Do you ever feel there are times where you are trying to prove yourself to someone? Do you consider your actions in these moments and what truly lies underneath the reasoning to prove yourself? Do you find yourself satisfied when others recognize your accomplishments, only to have that feeling be short lived? Take some time and write down your answers in your Integrity Vow Workbook.

I began to investigate the competitive aspects of myself and how they related to the cooperative aspects of me. I started learning more about feminine energy and embracing my own.

From what I have gathered and learned, modern society operates on mainly masculine energy. Some researchers indicate that most men work from a place of ninety-five percent masculine and five percent feminine. In the spiritual world, we look to create balance in our masculine and feminine energy and create our experiences from a place of cooperation rather than competition. This would not be an easy task at all but it made perfect sense. This energy is a correlation to ego and the circumstances that surrounded me had much to do with ego.

This can relate to self-help books and workshops as well. As we begin to understand change and see different results, often times we can try and control others by giving them the advice that we feel will help them. What we must remember is that everyone is on his or her own path. Everyone is at a different stage of self-discovery and this too is out of our control.

This applied to my home life. As my relationship continued with my wife, and we started discussing how to properly heal our family, I started trying to move her into a space of doing all the things that I was doing, and learning all the different knowledge that I was getting from coaching. I was telling her to read the books I was reading and do everything the same. This too was the wrong approach as everyone learns differently. My attempts to control her journey were impossible. I had to move to a place of understanding myself further and what my own truths were. She would do the same for herself and at her own pace.

The interesting part of this and a very resonating aspect of the Law of Attraction was that she began to do personal work for herself. I was letting go of the control in this case and my wife was starting to do some personal reading on her own. I'd see her post the odd spiritual quote online and she even visited a psychic. Something was there which she could learn from and I had nothing to do with pushing her towards that. Change was in the air for her regardless of the outcome of our relationship.

I no longer see things as I used to, which was primarily a projection of how I thought things were supposed to be. Instead I choose the realm of possibilities which allow me to find contentment and gratitude for all that is. This also provides a wonderful experience in that we come to understand the positive aspects of life, and that change is possible with the power of choice. This too gives us hope.

I found that in order to do this I needed to look at all of the circumstances that surrounded the two of us and stop trying to control everything. The push to control every situation or emphasize that I needed to control every situation was a pattern I had my entire life. In order to change my life, I needed to be free of that pattern.

Most of my coaching clients enter into my coaching program without understanding all of the roles that they are playing in day-to-day life. They don't recognize what their own experiences have created in them and why their current circumstances are the way that they are.

The initial discovery in this is not one of the more challenging aspects of self-discovery. The challenge is uncovering the truth about why we play the roles that we play day in and day out. As I take my clients through their own process of self-discovery, finding and embracing a deep understanding and truth about themselves, it can often be very painful. It is painful to look at the self and uncover who we are and the truth behind what we have come to be. It is important to be as transparent as possible, which is difficult at times due to the state of feeling vulnerable.

The wonderful part of this is that once we can embrace all of the parts of ourselves, and we determine the truth about our own story and values and what integrity means to us, we begin to make many more clear and positive choices.

Many times this can have a direct impact on the choices to betray a loved one or stay in a relationship where one has been betrayed. It can impact all of our choices in regards to relationships and circumstances, hopefully before we make unhealthy decisions.

Universal Law of Relativity

I believe this law resonates well with this chapter as it indicates and shows us that everyone experiences challenges and tests and that they all allow us to discover the personal power that lies within each and every one of us.

In order to truly evolve on our spiritual journey we must embrace these challenges, understand our own truths, and grow from a place of transparency.

Without the contrast that has been created in our own individual experiences, we would never be able to differentiate ourselves or evolve and expand.

Our experience here on earth would be quite mundane if we never had the opportunity to learn and grow as individuals. We would never understand how energy works and how the powerful Universal Laws apply to our experiences. We would never have a need to direct our energy with intention and attract the happiness, freedom and joy that we desire. We would never evolve.

The contrast that is often created from our previous experience is an opportunity for us to learn, gain knowledge and grow as spiritual beings. It is also an opportunity to find fulfillment in all areas of our lives.

The Law of Relativity shows us that these opportunities always show up to teach us what we have not yet come to learn. We must embrace these challenges and face our deepest truths further. This too allows us to learn about our powerful integral-selves.

What I love about this law is that it allows us to further understand other Universal Laws such as detachment. We begin to realize what is truly important to our own individual evolution, and to find happiness and freedom in healthy outcomes.

More often than not we come to discover that the real outcome we desire is one of spiritual growth and positive well-being. The negative or unhealthy attachments that we have to certain outcomes soon dissolve much more easily as we understand the truth about ourselves further.

I hope that you begin to embrace this law as you start to discover more about yourself, the truth about who you are and how integrity feels to you. Always remember that all is well and you are exactly where you need to be.

CHAPTER 7 EXERCISES

I am certain that those who achieve the best results in committing to this work are the ones who are the most transparent throughout the process. Consider these exercises in your own discoveries about truth and transparency. The answers will provide great insight to you.

1. In examining your current relationships with other people, do you feel that there is any lack of truth or transparency that pertains to them?
2. Where in your life are you not being as transparent as you could be?
3. Why do you think that is?
4. What would be the possible outcomes if you shared your truth?
5. Are there times in your life or even in your current experience that you feel you are not being truthful with yourself? Journal all of your answers in the Integrity Vow Workbook.

CHAPTER 8
Grace and Gratitude

"You were born a child of light's wonderful secret —
you return to the beauty you have always been"

—ABERJHANI

I'VE BEEN ASKED SEVERAL TIMES in my life what I'm thankful for. I can honestly say that there have been times when I felt I did not have an answer to that question.

I could see and feel some of the positive aspects that I was experiencing in life, but I was too attached and addicted to the negative aspects to feel any sense of true gratitude.

I'll admit that I can recall times when I was not practicing gratitude, even towards my own family. This too was an opportunity to reflect, learn and evolve further.

This chapter focuses on the principles of gratitude and how finding appreciation in all of our experiences is an integral part of healing the broken and tormented parts of ourselves. It will also discuss how we as humans can invoke grace into our experiences, which profoundly affects all of our outcomes.

This part of the book will focus on finding grace and gratitude in every situation that we encounter, which will heighten our emotional awareness and raise our overall vibration. There is always something to be grateful for and as we come to recognize this we begin to work with the Universal Law of Allowing.

The Law of Allowing teaches us that by understanding ourselves and finding grace and gratitude for all that we have created, we begin to evolve naturally and without resistance. It will be a wonderful law for you to work with on a regular basis.

Consider the notion that negative emotions such as fear, jealousy, anger, resentment or sadness cannot possibly exist when we are experiencing and tuning into the feeling of gratitude. It is simply impossible.

You may have heard this before, but if you cannot feel gratitude in your current experience, consider visiting a children's hospital or homeless shelter. I assure you that it won't take more than seconds to realize that your life has many blessings that you may not be fully recognizing or appreciating.

Have you come to understand that you are a reflection of every single choice that you have ever made? Do you recognize that every experience you are encountering is a direct result of those choices? Can you find a way to feel gratitude and give thanks for each experience you have encountered or whatever you may be currently going through? You have the power to understand this in an instant when you invoke grace and gratitude into your life.

As you begin to understand the power of gratitude, you will start to recognize that our thoughts dictate our reality. Whatever situation you're currently experiencing, whether it is positive or negative, holds gifts for your spiritual growth, no matter how dark these experiences may currently seem to be.

I understand that there are circumstances where you might say, "How could I make the choice to be in that car accident?" You might also ask more severe questions such as, "How could I choose to be raped or have a child die?" The pain and horrific feelings that these potentially devastating situations can cause are undeniable. I also understand that at times it feels impossible to find gratitude for experiences such as these.

I have not experienced everything that you may have. We all have our own unique circumstances that vary from person to person. What I do understand is that each of us made a choice one way or another. We made a choice to get into that car. We made a choice to have the child. We made a choice to walk down that dark alley where danger may have lurked. In other words, every single experience we created was based on our own personal choice.

This is not to minimize certain situations whatsoever. What I hope to bring your attention to is that there is great power in understanding and recognizing that we are a reflection of all of our choices, and that by owning the decisions we have made we can find gratitude for all of the experiences that have resulted. Easier said than done at times, but my intention is to show you how.

We didn't always choose the outcome of those choices, but we made a choice that caused us to experience an outcome. This is the lesson in personal responsibility and it applies directly to gratitude as well.

For every choice we make there is an outcome, and out of every outcome there is an opportunity to learn, grow and evolve. Even in the darkest of our experiences, there is an opportunity to grow. Sometimes it's just far more challenging to find the light in the darkness that may seem to surround us.

When I first began my spiritual journey I couldn't find anything in the present to be thankful for. It was ridiculous really, considering I had a home, three beautiful boys and a wife that was attractive, supportive, honest, and had more integrity than I can hope to have in a lifetime. She offered so much to our family that I had been taking for granted. I had success in work and many friendships that I had created over the years. For whatever reason, it didn't seem to be enough for me. I was always seeking more.

It wasn't enough to consider what I was experiencing in the current moment either, as far as what I wanted to be thankful for. I had to look at all of my experiences in life and seek gratitude for each and every one of them. This was a deep examination into my own personal background and history, which required a heightened state of awareness.

As I peeled back the layers of my life and started determining what was happening and why it was happening, I had to find grace and gratitude in every situation. I cannot say at all that I did this right away, but slowly and surely I began to find aspects of each and every situation I had encountered that I began to understand and find thanks in.

The first reflection was certainly my wife. I had made the choice to marry her. I had made the choice to have an affair despite being married to her. She had made the choice to give me an opportunity to become a better man for her and for our children. She had also given me the opportunity to become a better man for myself. When it came to my own infidelity, I'm thankful I was granted some grace to discover myself further while we remained married.

One of my long term coaching clients was married at the time I was going through my affair and ended up in a similar situation. He had two children and a similar story where he decided to seek fulfillment outside of his marriage.

It wasn't long after he stepped out of his integrity that the affair was discovered by his wife. That marriage ended instantly and he feels as though he is better off not being married. He felt that someone else would make him happier.

With love and respect, I don't judge him for this, as that's simply how our societal programming creates our attachments to certain outcomes. I truly believe that most marriages might survive more often if people learned how to do deep-rooted personal work and soul servicing before they made the decision to enter into a lifelong commitment. I watched him enter relationships with several other women that repeatedly ended in a similar fashion.

You see happiness ultimately lies within. There is no relationship that will create this experience for you other than the one that you have with your own integral-self. His point of attraction never changed as he had not made the decision to understand what his true integrity felt like. As he began to discover this, he finally decided to stop entering into relationships until he got clear on himself. His life has changed dramatically since making this discovery.

Ultimately, grace is a divine aspect of mercy. It allows us to impact Karma, create new outcomes, instantly change our behaviour and feelings, and heal the relationships with not only others but ourselves. It was when I began to invoke grace for others that I began to transform myself. It would require compassion, empathy, mercy, unconditional love and forgiveness.

The grace that my wife granted me has been unparalleled in my own life experience. I am forever grateful to her. She is a true warrior and she deserves more credit and recognition than I could ever provide her. She was a rock. She was a mother. She was a friend and she was true. When I reflect back on her, she's the purest person I have encountered.

Often times I wondered if being a father was the right path for me in life. It sounds strange, but domestication was a true challenge when I was initially married. Having our first child completely altered my life, and to be honest I didn't handle it well. I loved him with all my heart, but I was caught in a conflict between the previous freedom I was accustomed to as a single man and what I perceived as my new found responsibilities. I now realize how amazingly blessed I am to be a father of three wonderful boys.

I also believe I resented the responsibility because of the impact it had on my relationship with my wife. I didn't understand or have the tools to cope with that when we first got married, and the distance that parenting can create is something we just weren't aware of through the process of raising our first child.

This created more distance, and problems ensued. Our second child arrived two years later and I noticed the discord inside of our marriage throughout the process. We were now two parents with two children and neither of us had focused on keeping our relationship front and centre. The difference was that my wife still maintained integrity inside of our marriage, while clearly mine began to wane.

A third child was never in the plan for me. It was a confusing time in my life as we could both feel ourselves growing apart, and challenges and issues became more and more prevalent in our relationship. My wife did not have the same feelings and she maintained she wanted to try for a little girl, even though I completely resisted the idea. Instead of embracing the love and the joys that children bring to our world, I became unkind to her about her own wants and desires.

I began to resent her and it created major challenges in our marriage. Despite this, I was thrilled when our third son was born four years later. I just didn't know how to cope. I didn't know how to be grateful at the time in the entire manner that I should have been. It sounds cold, I realize. Who wouldn't be grateful for three wonderful children bringing joy and tremendous energy into the world? I can honestly say that for a time...I was that man.

I did shift this perception though, by invoking both grace and gratitude. Much of the anxiety and resentment was immediately interrupted anytime I found gratitude for my family. When I did, my world opened up. I was able to gain a sense of pride and accomplishment as I moved towards becoming a better father. Even when I was in an unhealthy relationship, my children kept me grounded enough to know the difference between right and wrong, and helped me to focus on what was truly important in life, which is love. I admit that I didn't see this clearly at times, but the bond that I have with them created a part of my awareness.

Relationships between husbands and wives can often change. The resilient relationships often adapt and to the various stages of life. The incredible relationships embrace them and enjoy them, knowing that they won't last forever and they are grateful for the time that they do have as being parents. I was fortunate to move into this space. I was fortunate to stop resisting this notion that my wife had told me all along. I am grateful that I recognized how important the family was and not just from a perceived level, but how important my family truly was to create a sense of joy in my life.

Another thing about love that is often overlooked or minimized is that it can provide an overwhelming sense of security at times. It is our duty as partners to recognize this. The centering and rhythm that my children provided me with ultimately kept me moving towards them, rather than away from them into unhealthy relationships. They were my guiding angels through my own life struggle as I did realize the integrity of maintaining my responsibility as a father, first and foremost. I moved away from resentment of responsibility and embraced it. I wish that I had done this sooner in my own personal parenting experience.

The gratitude I found for family was exactly what I needed, and really hit home with me. There was a sense of security and calmness when I was at home which was important to me for many years. I enjoyed being a father and taking my children to their sports and activities. There were many little moments I hadn't recognized before that I became more and more grateful for. All of my life I had been attracted to and created chaos and drama in most of my experiences. I was attracted to that, and yet the security of home, balance and a loving family were right there in front of me all along. I am forever thankful for this discovery about what it was that I truly wanted in life.

All we can do is our best in the circumstances that we are faced with. The spiritual path often does not recognize being with someone for the rest of your life as being the clearest path to enlightenment. While to some degree I can relate to this, I also challenge this notion as much of the research on Dharma that I have done places a great emphasis on purpose and serving family as purpose. We will discuss the Universal Law of Dharma and purpose more closely later on.

I cannot take back the decisions I made when my children were young. One day they may read this book and learn more about who their father was. I hope they do not experience life quite the same way I did. I hope the lessons they learn are a little bit easier than the ways in which I had to learn mine.

As a father, I will work relentlessly on protecting them and guiding them, as that is one of my greatest responsibilities. I cannot take back my past. I am grateful every day for the opportunity to make amends with the decisions I made and the opportunity to become a better man, and father. My children are indeed my most magical of creations. They are my ultimate manifestations in my own personal integrity. I am forever grateful for them.

What about you? Do you ever reflect on your experiences and realize all that you have to be grateful for? What can you find in your current experience to find thanks in? Can you find gratitude for the challenges you've faced or adversity you've overcome? Take a moment to reflect and journal your answers in the Integrity Vow Workbook.

Along the way I realized that the changes I was making in releasing my own addictions and attachments to certain relationships and some of the toxic aspects of myself gave me much to be grateful for. Sharing my story began to have a positive impact on other people's lives as well. This is another place where I found gratitude as it wasn't just that I was making changes, but that my friends and family were noticing. Of course, that was a nice feeling to experience, but there was more.

I noticed others were attracted to me as well, from afar, and even asked questions about the self-work that I was doing. This was the point when I realized I was beginning to embrace my darkness and shine some light on others. I didn't realize it at the time, but by coming from a place of transparency I was inspiring to many people. The more grace I found for all of my experiences, and the more I gave thanks for every aspect of my life, the more I found an abundance of others who were seeking similar changes for themselves.

As I began to learn more and work towards understanding the principles of personal discovery and integrity, I began to apply some of them inside of my coaching program. I am forever grateful to be granted the opportunity to help others with their personal growth. I ask that divine guidance flow through me to not only serve me, but to also serve and support others along the way.

I had to continue this path and walk the walk in order to do this at the highest level possible. Although I've reverted to form at times, my awareness remains a very high priority so that I can bring my best foot forward into each and every experience.

This is where I've found that alcohol and drug abuse, or other things that move me out of relationship integrity, no longer serve me or are choices that I ever wish to make again. I have not been perfect in this declaration, but even the occasional glass of wine moves me out of my true rhythm. It's different for everyone, but this is my own personal truth.

Consider your own experience for a moment and reflect on grace and gratitude. Are you making any choices in your experience that may alter your awareness and prevent you from realizing how much there is to be thankful for? Do the relationships you have with others affect your responsibility to find grace and gratitude in every experience? Write down your answers in the Integrity Vow Workbook.

We will discuss manifestation later in the book, but I must say that a clear mind is the healthiest way to make clear choices. When we make clear choices that are in integrity, we begin to create the experiences that we wish to have in every aspect of our lives. I am grateful for learning this and without the past experiences of addiction I would have never done so.

There is also much gratitude to give in regards to some of the adversity I encountered as a young man. Losing my childhood friend, Terri, who was someone I had so much love for at such a young age, was very traumatic for me. There are images that surround her death that will be forever ingrained in my mind. I hope that I never cry that hard again, but I am thankful to know what doing so feels like.

I am grateful that I got to know her. I am grateful that I was able to share a childhood with such a magnificent soul, full of pure energy and someone who only wanted good for this world. I am grateful that I had a friend to spend time with when I was very young as I believe it helped me get through some of the darkness of my parent's divorce, even if I didn't realize it at the time. I am grateful to have known such innocence in the world. I am grateful for the time Terri and I shared together when we were young.

She was a special human being who saw beneath the surface of appearances. It gave me confidence there was more to life than just the surface. It made me proud to have such a beautiful friend pay attention to me, especially when I wasn't getting very much attention anywhere else. I thank her for the laughs that we had when I needed them most, and for teaching me how to be myself. I cherish our past conversations and the time we spent together and the relationship we had as we both came of age. I have never had anyone who I felt was watching over me, but I know now that I have guidance from heaven.

All of the relationships we encounter in our lifetimes show up to teach us important lessons. I didn't always believe that, but learning about love and understanding is a valuable lesson. I know now that love from another human being is important to complement the more important aspect of loving ourselves. We can act as though we don't want to have that kind of committed partnership, but in the end the human need for love of ourselves and others prevails. When you begin to find gratitude for all of your relationship experiences in this manner, you begin to align with the ebb and flow of the Universe. People come and go but all hold tremendous gifts in each experience.

I need to express gratitude for being a child who was bullied in school. Those experiences appeared over the course of many years to show me I had low self-worth and needed to do the appropriate work on myself to heal. They appeared to teach me resiliency and also mental toughness since I had no support in this area as a child. I did not always respond to bullying responsibly and admittedly became a bully at times in my own life. However these too were lessons on how to allow myself to evolve, and to teach me what I needed to learn at those particular times in order to become a responsible human being.

Be sure to find gratitude for every experience and grant grace where grace is needed. Self-appreciate and find thanks for your own choices and decisions, whatever they may be. Extend grace not only to others but to yourself as needed.

I had a coaching client enter my program a little while ago who was having major marital challenges. She had begun an affair with a man who was using cocaine heavily and she began to find herself abusing drugs too. Although she had a young child, she began to find herself in her basement each night after her family was in bed snorting lines of coke. She was depressed, anxious and experiencing severe emotional pain.

Her original perspective when she began coaching with me was that she wanted to get a divorce. She felt that she had made a mistake in getting married and having a child. After several coaching calls she became unresponsive, and I soon found out that she had abandoned her family and flown to Thailand for a month alone.

After she had been there for about thirty days by herself, I received a call from her. She was confused as she felt she had made a mistake in leaving her family. The time away from her inappropriate relationship and her choice to refrain from drug use had given her a new perspective, that the security of family and home could be something she wanted after all.

I asked her if her husband was willing to work on the relationship and she indicated that he was. I then asked her if she took full responsibility for the choices that she had made leading up to abandoning her family. She indicated she had, although she was struggling with guilt and the shame involved from the experience she had created. She was worried about what everyone would think of her and how it would affect all areas of her life.

It was here that I coached her to look inwards and to find a deeper understanding of herself in order for her to self-discover and self-appreciate. The important choice she had made, although severe, gave her new found clarity and gratitude for not only her family but herself. We worked with the laws of grace and as she returned home, her husband agreed to give her a second chance. These laws are ever so powerful in what they can create when worked with in integrity.

I cannot predict whether her marriage will work out or not. The circumstances that appear in each one of our individual journeys is different for all of us. What I will state with certainty is that when we invoke grace and gratitude, we find ourselves in much different circumstances and we give ourselves an opportunity to create much better outcomes.

Until we understand that all of the power we are seeking is internal, we cannot make choices that allow us to experience grace or gratitude. This pertains to every single choice you will ever make for the rest of your life. Every single choice in the relationships and experiences that you have had are opportunities to grow. When you begin to experience your current circumstances from this perspective, you will understand how grace and gratitude will allow you to experience what you truly desire.

I want to reiterate that self-awareness is the key. Although we can find gratitude in the most negative of experiences, we must still exercise personal responsibility. Not every relationship with others is meant to continue.

Grace can exist in these circumstances too. We must be grateful for those experiences and the people involved and show mercy towards them, even if it's from a distance. We may not receive pleasant responses but supporting others with grace will do more for someone than resenting or trying to change them.

I will also note that there are times when we must be personally responsible and create boundaries with others. Much of the next chapter will address this topic. You will begin to work further with the Law of Association and understand what truly serves your integral-self. In each of your experiences, my hope is that you find gratitude for all of them, and grant grace where it is needed most.

There is always a choice to be made in every situation that you encounter. Consider times where you were applying for a job that you so desperately wanted and yet you were rejected. Often times, days or weeks later, a better job opportunity is presented to you. It is in circumstances like this that we must reflect and find gratitude. There is always a new and exciting outcome available to us if we allow ourselves to receive it.

The Universal Law of Allowing

Grace and gratitude are important factors to working with this law as it indicates we must allow things to evolve naturally and without resistance.

This is not always an easy law to work with as we have been programmed from such an early age to think and react a certain way to most of our experiences, rather than respond effectively. Remember that responding is rooted in personal responsibility.

The Universal Law of Allowing shows us that universal energy moves in a current-like flow. When we allow the Universe to work in its natural state, we create our experiences with ease and less resistance.

When we allow our experiences to shape us, rather than resisting what they appear to teach us about ourselves, we avoid interfering with the other powerful Laws of the Universe.

Most of us are trained and programmed to feel that we must react to every situation versus finding the gifts that exist in each and every experience we encounter. When we allow the Universe to work in its natural state, we can only then experience a pure form of manifestation or creation.

Often times we feel that we know better than the Universe, due to the way we were brought up or the experiences that taught us from an early age how things are supposed to be.

This is simply not the case. The Universe allows each experience we are supposed to have at each and every given moment. We feel the energy and vibration in all of our thoughts and experiences. When we learn to trust in Universal order and understand how the laws work, we can find thanks in many of the experiences we are faced with including the difficult and challenging ones.

Extending thanks to the Universe is also a choice and one that will allow you to begin making other choices in a free and desirable state. This is a state that will allow you to experience alignment and create an abundance of new outcomes that match your true desires and integral-self.

This law is the opposite of the Law of Resistance which we addressed earlier. Remember that what we resist persists and by trusting the gift of intuition, trusting the Universe, and ultimately finding gratitude for the ability to do so, you will begin to create experiences beyond your wildest dreams.

This possibility that you can experience everything that you desire is one hundred percent true for you and every other human being on the planet. My challenge to you is to understand where you have been in your life and what you are experiencing now, with a knowing that things will improve drastically if you make different choices.

So give thanks to the lessons and blessings that you've encountered. Grant grace where grace is needed to the people and circumstances that no longer serve you, and feel excitement for brighter days ahead. Allow yourself to experience your highest potential.

CHAPTER 8 EXERCISES

Exploring areas where you can grant grace and express gratitude will have a profound impact on your current experience. The following exercises will allow you to consider where grace and gratitude exist or are needed in your life.

1. List five things you are grateful for.
2. List five people or situations where you've found it difficult to grant grace, but where doing so would serve you well.
3. Write down any past circumstances where you have experienced pain, and ask yourself what you can now find gratitude in. Journal your answers in the Integrity Vow Workbook.

CHAPTER 9
Choices and Boundaries

"You are the average of the five people
that you associate with the most."

-JIM ROHN

WOULD YOU BELIEVE ME, IF I told you that you could feel your way through any situation? If you could increase your own awareness about all of your surroundings, do you feel like you would have a knowing as to what decisions you need to make in order to find the abundance and freedom you desire?

The choices we make in day-to-day life will shape all of our experiences, including the relationships we have with others. Whether you are someone who has participated in an inappropriate relationship, are considering involving yourself in one, or have had someone break their trust with you, the Law of Association and your point of attraction will offer you great gifts and guidance. It will also allow you to create new boundaries for yourself and your circumstances to ensure you stay in your highest place of integrity.

It is not always the people or circumstances however that we must understand. More often we require a clear understanding of the emotions we are experiencing and the vibration we are offering. This will have a direct impact on your relationships with others and yourself.

When I am feeling happy, I find myself making very productive choices with my friends, family and co-workers. If I am feeling sad, jealous or angry then I also understand how these negative emotions can affect me. When I came to understand these emotions and the energy associated with all of my feelings, I was able to begin offering a different vibration with just a simple change of perspective. This, along with the power of my own decision making, allowed me to change everything. You can do this too.

Rather than allowing myself to let my emotions control me, the feelings that I now encounter are a very informative guidance system to navigate all of my surroundings and experiences. I can literally decide what decisions will serve my higher purpose and most integral-self. I assure you that with this process of self-discovery you will be able to do the same, and with much more ease than you might imagine.

You will begin to determine and realize that all of the people and circumstances you are surrounded with are offering a vibration to you as well. You will feel this energy and know with clear certainty whether you want to continue in these experiences or whether perhaps you need to make different choices. The power is situated right within you to do so.

Although my affair had ended and I was living a very clean lifestyle, I continued to find myself experiencing various emotions that were overwhelming. These included guilt, shame, resentment, jealousy, sadness and even anger. Recognizing these feelings was a good practice in my own emotional awareness. I also began to create boundaries when it came to choices about who I would associate with, how I would spend my time, and even boundaries in regards to my thoughts and emotions.

This can be challenging at first, as many of the associations we have start out with good intentions but do not always serve the best version of ourselves. Sometimes the vibration that others offer can have an impact if we allow ourselves to absorb that energy into our own experience.

I began to notice this with friends, family and coworkers who, by all accounts, I had good relationships with. Although many of these relationships were not severely negative in nature, they still had an impact on my own experience that was not helping me find a higher vibration. I began to discover and understand that examining and changing some of my associations was necessary.

Some of my friends who had gone through a divorce or had unhealthy or unsatisfying relationships began to wear on my emotions. I realized that participating in conversations that were lower in vibration would not serve what I was hoping to accomplish at home.

There is a difference between social and business networking that became very clear to me. I realized that unless the meeting was strictly professional, I was giving someone my time and energy instead of my family. That did not serve my integral-self either and I had to make specific choices to create boundaries in these circumstances too.

Many of my clients discover that they must make similar choices to create boundaries. The challenge that exists for them and many others is often that they are highly productive in business, however their quality of life is suffering outside of their chosen careers. They are directing more energy to their business rather than serving purpose or their families.

One of the first exercises that I take all of my clients through is a time study that allows them to self-discover not only the way that they are spending their time, but more importantly, the choices that they are making inside of that time. I have included this in your Integrity Vow Workbook.

Consider this study for yourself:

1. Write down the number 168 on paper.
   There are 168 hours available to each and every single one of us in any week. This is no different for any other human being on the planet. It is the way that we spend that time and the choices that we make from a place of personal responsibility

that dictate what the outcome of our time spent looks like. Instead of time management, begin to consider the notion of choice management.

2. Sleep Hours

Identify and write down the number of hours on average that you sleep in a week. There is no wrong answer here so I ask that you are as transparent as possible. There are great discoveries when you analyze your sleep time. It is important to maintain a healthy and optimal level of rest, however oversleeping can severely impact your productivity. Remember that we are never tired when we are inspired.

3. Subtract this number from your original 168 hours.

4. Work Hours

Write down the number of hours on average that you dedicate to your career in a week. For some of you it may be forty hours, and others of you, it may be sixty or eighty hours. Again, there are no wrong answers here.

5. Subtract this number from your remaining time.

6. Personal or Spiritual Development Time

Next I want you to write down the number of hours on average that you dedicate to yourself. This is what I refer to as personal or spiritual development time, and it can be anything for you that will allow you to bring your best self forward into each and every experience. Perhaps it's fitness and nutrition, or possibly journaling and meditation. It can even be going for a walk or reading a non-business related book. In my deepest truth and my most integral-self I am certain that we cannot serve other human beings, including our spouses, children, friends, family and clients, until we serve ourselves at the highest level possible. I hope that by now you have come to agree with this.

7. Personal or Spiritual Development Commitment

Subtract ten hours, which you will now make a commitment to dedicating to yourself each week, from your total hours remaining.

8. After you subtract your sleep hours, work hours and personal or spiritual development time from your original 168 hours, how many hours do you have left?

   Most people will have anywhere between thirty and fifty hours per week left over once they dedicate themselves to sleeping, working and serving themselves first. This identifies that there is plenty of time to serve other human beings and to also work with purpose.

9. Time Allocation

   This remaining amount of time is the time that I want you to dedicate first and foremost each and every week. This is the time we dedicate with purpose and intention.

You see, we all have plenty of time to do the things we want to do with the people we want to do them with. The time study above will show you that you have all the time in the world — at least more than you might currently recognize — and it is available for you. The reason I want you to dedicate your purposeful time first is that it will allow you to be responsible and avoid what we have come to know as "career resentment." In all of this we can begin to realize that we dictate how this time is spent with the choices we make in our own experience.

The reason I want you to dedicate the time spent on your personal or spiritual development second, which usually becomes your most important priority, is that it will allow you to get more intentional. As you continue to self-discover and dedicate yourself to the spiritual path, you will begin to see a positive spillover effect in all areas of your life.

Whatever your chosen career path is, and with a knowing that it may change one day, I assure you that it is very rarely going to be your life's purpose. In the real estate environment I work in, I've come to understand that nobody is going to wake up one day on death's doorstep indicating that their life would have been far more fulfilling and complete, if they had only sold one more house.

Business or a career is nothing more than a vehicle. It is a vehicle to do the things we want to do with the people we want to do them with. It is a way to serve our purpose, which can be anything for you once you discover it. Perhaps it's your family or maybe it pertains to serving a charity of your choice that you are passionate about. In my own experience, and after many years of working without any purpose, I came to understand that my purpose is contributing to other human beings through my coaching, speaking and writing. In our next chapter, we will discover purpose even further and apply the Universal Law of Dharma, however for the moment let's continue investigating time and the choices that we make inside of our available time.

There are wonderful answers if you take an honest approach and look at your time using the exercise above. Almost all of my one-on-one clients quickly realize that it's not the lack of time that is getting in the way of the happiness, freedom or integral-selves that they desire. More often than not it has to do with the choices that they make inside of that time.

Let's revisit Free Will for a second or two...

As human beings we have all been granted free will and the ability to make choices. As we've come to understand from earlier chapters, many of the choices that I made in my own experience provided wonderful opportunities to learn and grow spiritually and evolve my integral-self. Some of these experiences were very painful and destructive, however there were gifts in each and every one of them.

It is when we come to understand that in order to experience our true integral-selves, along with the happiness and freedom that we desire, we must work diligently with the Universal Law of Action and the Universal Law of Intention. You see, as we discover our purpose we begin to make choices that reflect just that. As we begin to get more purposeful, we then start to take action and line up our choices, which in essence are actions with our intentions. As we begin to get more intentional, we begin to get more impactful, and although we don't always see it immediately, the choices we make with intention often create the results that we truly desire.

Every single choice we make inside of the time we have available to us in our 168 hours of free time will have a result. This is a reflection of the free will that has been granted to us as human beings. This applies to every area in our lives, including the way we spend our time, how we choose to treat our bodies and nourish our minds, the people we decide to spend time with, and even the thoughts we choose to think about.

Everything is a result and reflection of our own free will.

As you begin to discover some of the choices you make inside of your time, I want you to pause and reflect on critical areas which will serve your most integral-self. The first is the Universal Law of Association.

The Universal Law of Association indicates that we become like an average of the five people we surround ourselves with the most. In this chapter you will determine who those five people are for you. You can write your responses to the following discussion in your Integrity Vow Workbook, or you can wait until the end of the chapter where I have summarized it in the exercise section.

I will also ask that you consider what kind of vibration each one of those five offers and what each person's point of attraction is. Remember the point of attraction that you are experiencing with each other person is almost always the one that you are currently offering yourself. Like attracts like, which again is Universal Law.

As spiritual beings that have been put on this earth in order to learn, grow and evolve in our human experience, this law is of utmost importance. In order to evolve we must begin to surround ourselves with people that are going to serve us at a higher level than we have previously experienced.

This pertains to business, family, relationships, spirituality or anything to do with the positive experience that we wish to create in our lives. We must identify our surroundings and investigate the possibility that we may want to seek others on different paths than the ones that we have grown accustomed to.

Our society, and often times various religions, program us to consider our surroundings as normal and acceptable. We are taught that being average is often times better than being different, which ultimately creates nothing more than mediocrity.

Our souls know different however, because we are spiritual beings that were created long before the societal programming happened to us when we were children. It is our free will that allows us to discover this further, and an awareness to make this choice is crucial to your own evolution and growth.

Are the people you are associating yourself with influencing your spiritual, professional or personal growth and evolution? Again, take a look at your circle and pose the question about the five people you spend the most time with. You can also take this a step further and apply it to the various areas of your life that you want to focus on.

If you are hoping for greater productivity in business, perhaps you want to discover and explore the five people that you surround yourself with inside of your career. Are they having an influence on your productivity and income?

If it is your own spiritual growth, perhaps you want to consider the relationships you have with your immediate circle and consider whether or not they are truly going to allow you to grow and determine what integrity means to you. Of course it is your choice to surround yourself with these people, and the most amazing aspect of this is that you can make different choices and create different surroundings at any time.

If you are in an inappropriate relationship, are you conscious of the vibration that the partner you are having an affair with is offering? If you are considering infidelity, does your environment impact the decision you are about to make? If you have been cheated on and are trying to find your own resolve, are your surroundings supporting your growth in this regard?

In order to work closely with and make the most of this powerful Universal Law, it is incredibly important to begin considering what your boundaries are as well. Do you need to create different relationships with co-workers, friends or family members? More often than not, you will also want to ask yourself if there are new boundaries that need to be established and created in order to experience new outcomes. Here are some initial steps to working with this law:

1. Consider your current associations and ask yourself if you are associating with people who have a positive impact on your life.

2. Consider the notion of cooperation and competition. It is not always ideal to be the "best" in your own five associations. In order to grow, we must learn from the experiences of others and I recommend finding those that have great experience in the areas you wish to improve in. Surround yourself with these people and learn from them regularly.

3. Create boundaries, which unfortunately may mean that you will need to disassociate with anyone who is having a negative impact in your life. This is not always easy to do, but the reward in losing something you currently perceive as negative will be a positive experience in the long run.

4. Ask yourself what areas of your life you wish to change and begin looking for other associations which may serve you in this growth.

5. Toxic relationships have to end. I can't simplify this any further and it's imperative to your growth.

6. Revisit your associations frequently and apply the process outlined above.

It is only when we heal ourselves that we can begin to heal others. Healing is different for everyone and it requires a lot of effort and focus to fully heal. Before I could try to heal my marriage I had to focus my efforts inward to be able to bring myself into alignment with my own integrity. It was self-discovery that would allow me to realize the choices I had been making in regards to my surroundings, and the boundaries I would need to create to improve my own experience.

A dedicated path of awareness allowed me to understand myself and discover past programming and patterns. The path of personal responsibility allowed me to make new choices to serve my higher and most integral-self.

Free will had created all of those previous experiences. This went as far back into my childhood, teen years and young adulthood, and would create all of my future outcomes. This was a painful process in some cases, however recognizing the choices I had made and allowing myself to feel that pain was an integral part of my own self-discovery. This process also began to allow me to create boundaries when it came to my emotional choices.

I began to develop new methods that went beyond just invoking grace and gratitude as discussed in the previous chapter. This was a process and a way of creating a new normal with an increased sense of awareness and self-worth. This is a very dedicated path that will require ongoing commitment and awareness on your journey if you truly want to step into the highest version of yourself.

There was no possible way that our marriage would begin to heal if I did not only start, but also continue, doing this work. If I did not walk the path of my most integral-self it would be too easy to continually revert to form and my old ways. We can't just suppress the painful parts of us, as they always exist, however an understanding and allowing process will ensure these parts guide us to better outcomes.

It was crucial to understand this as I wanted to ensure that I did not revert to making more poor choices. I will not say it's been a perfect process, however a heightened state of awareness certainly served me in identifying the tests that continually occur in life. Those universal tests exist for all of us. Recognizing these moments is such an integral part of making healthy choices and utilizing free will, along with establishing new boundaries when necessary.

You see, many will begin the journey of self-discovery, and like other things in life, they start a project however they don't complete it. Looking at yourself is the most difficult thing you can ever do as it uncovers parts of yourself that don't necessarily feel good to see.

It can be painful, and it's very easy to understand why people bury those feelings with escape mechanisms such as addictions and attachments, or perhaps by having an affair. It is imperative that we recognize that the unhealthy emotions and attachments we encounter are there to serve us in making different choices with free will, rather than letting them control our actions to create more unhealthy outcomes. This too is an aspect of personal responsibility.

Free will is present at all times and in every moment of the day. This also pertains to our emotions and the way that we choose our thoughts. Emotions such as sadness, jealousy, judgment and rage will drastically change the way that we make our own choices. The same is true when we make choices with love, compassion, sympathy and empathy.

What we are seeking to understand is how to use free will to create healthier outcomes. By understanding our surroundings and creating clear boundaries when it comes to our associations, circumstances and emotions, we begin to create much more desirable experiences.

This is why it is so important to understand how Universal Laws will impact every choice you continue to make in your life. Creating balance and minimizing some of the negative and toxic emotions that exist within you will allow you to fully trust in the way that the Universe works.

Begin to create emotional boundaries for yourself and stay aware of the choices you are making based on the way you feel in any given moment. Ask yourself when negative emotions arise whether you are making choices based on responsibility, or reacting to a person, trigger or any situation. There is a dramatic difference in what you will create.

In understanding your own integrity you will begin to utilize free will in a way that serves you at a much higher level than ever before. You are the one who gets to make these choices and our goal is to make the most beneficial choices possible at all times.

It is also important to understand that the Law of Association and the boundaries we create with people, places, circumstances and our own emotions has nothing to do with anyone else, but everything to do with you.

It is crucial that we do not judge others for the decisions that they make with their own free will. Instead we must observe others with empathy, compassion and love. It is important to be fully detached from the outcomes that others create for themselves.

Remember that judgment often has much to do with how we project ourselves onto others, along with creating an experience whereby we try to control circumstances that are completely out of our own control.

The free will that others exercise is for them and we will never be able to control the choices anyone else makes. As you study and create more of your outcomes, applying all of the ideas, insights and Universal Laws in this book, you will begin to understand this more and more. Life becomes easier when you detach from the experiences of others.

Pause for a moment and consider your integral-self and what that truly means to you. Are you creating the experiences that you desire with your own free will? Are your surroundings having a positive or negative impact on your current experience? Have you created appropriate boundaries with your external circumstances and internal emotions? Are you walking an authentic path or are you portraying an identity that does not truly feel authentic to you? Journal your answers in your Integrity Vow Workbook.

If you have come to understand that your current experience is a reflection of all of your previous choices, you may begin to ask yourself how to change some of the direction that you are currently having based on your own free will.

Almost all of the experiences I have discussed in this book, whether they belong to me, my coaching clients or most of the people on this planet, have to do with low self-esteem. We each must discover how our experiences led to our own particular sense of low self-worth.

My story involves many experiences where low self-worth was created. Based on the relationship I had with my parents, being bullied as a kid, previous relationships and challenges with my weight as a child, my self-esteem was something that was in need of great repair.

I would not have known where to begin with this process as I had been programmed that way from an early age and had no foundation for creating a new standard of self-worth. I had to find a new way of living and a life that would allow me to bring a different experience forward, not only for myself but for my family and those around me. I certainly would never want my children to experience low self-worth in the same way that I had. Of course, I now express gratitude as what I've learned from those experiences allows me to serve my children in a positive way.

As I now do with most of the people who coach with me, I began to investigate my own associations and seek out various guides that would support me in increasing my own sense of self-worth and developing a strong sense of emotional awareness. The original coach who I began working with was a high level businessman and a national bodybuilding competitor who I felt would serve me well. I also began to work with energy and emotional guides, spiritual coaches and a creative coach. It took time to discover the associations that would serve me and why I would require new associations and mentors or guides.

My first coach placed an emphasis on fitness and nutrition at the beginning of the coaching process, and I typically do the same with all of my own coaching clients. Although I didn't realize it at the time, this would be a crucial part of building a new foundation and increasing my own self-esteem. I continue to work with guides and mentors that assist with my commitment and consistency in this space.

The late Wayne Dyer said it well, "Nurture the body and you will nurture the soul." This didn't resonate at first, but it became one of the most important aspects of my spiritual journey. What he speaks of here, and what I reference with my own clients, is of a self-serving nature, but in a positive way. This includes working out, proper diet and nutrition, reading, meditation, energy healing, and all sorts of other rituals that we will continue to explore. By utilizing my own free will, I learned to make new choices in every aspect of my life, which also created some new time boundaries to serve myself at a higher level.

I began a ninety day process of creating these healthy choices and boundaries in every area of my life. This had to do with everything this chapter explains: examining my associations with other people, commitment to time and understanding the choices I was making with my time, energy and emotions. I was not attached to any outcome at the end of ninety days other than feeling healthier and happier.

This was perfect timing as I had ceased all contact with the woman I had entered into an inappropriate relationship with. I had some lingering negative emotions towards not only her, but myself, that I wanted to further resolve. I had been limiting my alcohol consumption, but I wanted to create a stronger boundary with my relationship and association with drinking as well. This too would place a positive boundary with my emotions as alcohol, after all, is a depressant.

It wasn't easy and it required willpower, however every time I thought about getting drunk, I made a conscious decision not to. I had recognized the power of choice when it pertained to alcohol, and utilizing it was a crucial aspect of my own personal responsibility.

I was seeing progress as I began to work out and eat healthier. I decided I didn't want to stay on the roller coaster where I would work hard all week and then blow all my progress over the weekend. I had done that enough and wanted to see a different kind of result. I also started to recognize the relationship with alcohol and my emotional well-being. This began to have a positive impact with my emotions and the outcomes I was creating.

"Nurture the body, nurture the soul." It was like a mantra at the beginning. It was almost like an addiction because the workouts created a euphoric feeling when my endorphins were released, and that gave me a sense of relief. The results did not come immediately or as quickly as I was hoping, however I began to see progress and feel better. That was all that mattered when I got started: just feeling better. I didn't walk into a dark forest overnight and I certainly wasn't going to walk out overnight either, but I started to see some light at the end of the tunnel.

After six weeks I began to notice results. I went from 197 pounds to 180 pounds. This was pretty dramatic, as I was also changing the composition of my body substantially. Most of this came from working out regularly and eliminating alcohol. I was not fully committed to nutrition at the time and wanted more results and an even healthier outcome. It was with a commitment to a new association, with someone who had a greater experience and results in the physical arena, that I began to understand the importance of health and nutrition and what that meant to me. By utilizing my own free will and making wiser choices, I also created time boundaries where working out became a non-negotiable part of my life.

Working out is one thing, but what most people fail to realize is that nutrition is ninety percent of the success when it comes to our physical health. It's also the most daunting. Think about it this way: we can commit to sixty to ninety minute workouts, but that is such a small portion of the day. Nutrition requires us to remain aware, and to dedicate time or money to ensure we eat the proper foods that will fuel our bodies all day long. Hence, it is a much more dedicated commitment.

Healthy nutrition is crucial, and it consumes the entire day. The choices we have are abundant, to promote a healthy physical transformation or not. We are constantly tempted by unhealthy foods. With all the advertising and media, the next poor choice is always right at the tips of our fingers. Our society is one that celebrates with food and alcohol, and these days there are constant celebrations. Once again, we can invoke our own free will and create boundaries with food and nutrition.

I had to make the choice to step outside of what was normal. My friends, family, children and co-workers all had different positions and habits when it came to healthy eating. I needed to make the choice for myself to do what was right for me in this space alone. This was my own choice to make and a dedication to my integral-self. I began eating six meals per day, each consisting of one protein, one carbohydrate and one green vegetable.

The key in health and wellness is to ask yourself whether you are truly committed or not. Understand that you have the choice to change your decisions at any time. Even the healthiest of body builders or professional athletes fall off track from time to time, but the difference is how they choose to recommit. They understand what they need to do and the choices that they must make. They find their own associations for evolving in their respective spaces, and the difference-maker for most of them is that they are very responsible when it comes to the choice of maintaining consistency.

Here's a short commitment exercise that I used and continue to use on a daily, weekly, and monthly basis, which I learned from one of my mentors and apply with my own coaching clients:

1. What was my commitment?
2. Did I reach my commitment?

3. In the realm of all that was possible, could I have reached my commitment?
4. What got in the way?
5. Do I want to recommit?
6. What did I learn about myself from this experience?
7. Acknowledgement for those commitments that I kept.

Notice number 4 for a moment. It is not our friends, family, clients or relationships that usually get in the way of us maintaining and reaching our commitments. More often than not, it is ourselves and what we do with our own free will and choices.

THE LAW OF ASSOCIATION

This law indicates that we become like the average of the five people we surround ourselves with the most and can have a dramatic influence on the experiences we create.

In understanding and recognizing how this law impacts your own experience, I've asked you to relate your associations to all of your desired outcomes.

Your associations could be for the purpose of your career, family, friends, spiritual development, and your own integrity. The discoveries in this law will give you guidance on what associations you may currently have and whether change is in order for you.

It is crucial to recognize the importance of creating associations that will promote your growth rather than hinder it. This applies to all of your surroundings and desires.

CHAPTER 9 EXERCISES

The choices that you make inside of the time you have available and the people that you spend your time with will have a dramatic impact on that which you wish to experience. Pay close attention to your discoveries as you complete these chapter exercises.

1. Complete the 168-hour time study provided to you at the beginning of this chapter. Journal your answers in the Integrity Vow Workbook.
2. Identify the five people that you surround yourself with the most in your life.
3. Journal about the vibration that you are offering them, and the vibrations they are offering to you.
4. List three areas of your life where you desire change and consider the Law of Association and what choices you may need to make in order to create the growth and evolution that you desire.

Honour and Temptation

"But if it be a sin to covet honour, I am
the most offending soul alive."

-WILLIAM SHAKESPEARE

HAVE YOU BEEN READING THIS book and finding that you are discovering more and more about yourself? Perhaps you're still unsure about what direction to take in certain parts of your spiritual and physical experience. Have you come to understand that everything that you want to create is completely possible as long as you are staying aware of your true integral-self and you are making appropriate and responsible choices? Are you still challenged by certain aspects, or are you perhaps feeling fearful of making changes to step further into your own experience of integrity? Are you so close to that true integral breakthrough, yet still uncertain that you're honouring your own path?

One of my favourite definitions of honour is as follows:

Honour means doing what you believe to be right and being confident that you have done what is right.

Although there are many definitions of honour, what I love about this one is the notion that you are doing what you feel is right rather than doing what someone *else* feels is right. It is a self-empowering mindset to find courage and build your own sense of self-worth.

The societal programming and the experiences of low self-worth that are often created in our lives can be challenging at best. Often this may lead to us questioning ourselves on the decisions we make and the way others may perceive us. This can have a dramatic impact on our own conscience, which can be very paralyzing and confusing. Conscience can be very fear based, which we will continue to explore.

What I want you to recognize is that this life is yours, and only you get to decide how to honour your own journey. Of course we must be responsible for all of our choices, however we often worry too much about the opinions of others. My hope is that you do not become too consumed in a life that traps you to a societal standard that does not satisfy you.

An American university conducted an exercise called "The Funeral Study" years ago. This was designed to poll the opinions of people in regards to how much the opinions of others influenced their choices. The implications and results allow us to discover purpose further.

Fifty percent of all the people you know will attend your funeral, and of those people, only one third will attend your funeral if it is raining.

There are many other studies like this that allow us to discover that we get so needlessly consumed in what others think about our lives. Ultimately, people are so caught up in their own lives that they don't pay as much attention to ours as we think they do. Why do we continue to worry about the opinions of others and opt not to honour our own?

Of course I'm not implying that we should behave in ways that are dishonest, harmful or malicious, however we must understand that we only have one life to live. The choices that we make with our own free will are just that: our choices. When we honour ourselves and our own life path, we begin to find happiness and freedom like never before.

There are also opportunities that the Universe will continue to present you with in order for you to honour your own path of integrity. These may appear as people, relationships, circumstances or quick decisions that you must make in order to maintain your integrity-based path.

One of my coaching clients entered my program after she heard me speak at a seminar where I applied some of the Universal Law applications that we've discussed in this book. She explained early on in the process that the Law of Association resonated with her as she had entered into an inappropriate relationship with a colleague at work.

Although she had not been physically intimate with her colleague, she was very emotionally attached to him since they'd worked closely together for several years.

Early on in their working relationship they found themselves spending a great deal of time together before, during and after work hours where they would engage in conversations about work, their relationships, and life in general.

They became very close to one another and at various times in the first several years of working together, they expressed an attraction to one another. This attraction was beyond the normal and responsible aspect of working together. For whatever reason, they didn't overstep the physical boundary, however a clear attraction was evident. She indicated that they both expressed fear to one another regarding crossing boundaries.

She was married at the time with two young children and was struggling inside her marital relationship. Her colleague was also in a relationship in which he lived with another woman, however he indicated he was feeling unfulfilled at home.

I asked her how she would feel if her husband found out that she was spending so much time with another man. How would he feel if he walked into the restaurants they had dinner at, or coffee shops where they spent time together? What would be his response if he witnessed them in deep emotional engagement? How would she feel if she walked into the same restaurants and coffee shops and witnessed her husband having this type of interaction with one of his co-workers?

My client became very confused. She indicated that she loved her husband and although there were good times in her marriage, the recent years had been a struggle for them and they had even discussed divorce. She was in an emotional state of turmoil on what to do about her marriage and whether or not she should end her relationship to explore something more with her colleague.

From previous chapters we have come to understand that making serious decisions when we have strong emotional attachments or addictions to other people is very challenging and not recommended. How can we make such a decision that holds such a powerful impact? This is especially true when marriage and children are involved. In this chapter we are exploring relationships and the ongoing tests and temptations that become present in our lives. We are also addressing how working with the Universal Law of Dharma and purpose can have a profound impact in helping you clear this ambivalence, and honour your choice to maintain your highest and most integral-self. This will allow you to create more desirable outcomes and create self-appreciation and a greater sense of pride.

Often we find ourselves in circumstances where we must make challenging decisions. In order to make appropriate and responsible choices, utilizing the powerful Universal Laws and understanding our emotions are crucial for success.

Are we working from a place of fear in what others would think of the consequences of our actions, or are we working in purpose with confidence and an inner knowing that we are in integrity? The Universe will continually present these questions to each and every one of us.

My coaching client had been receiving some additional input from several spiritual guides who she enjoyed learning from. She worked with a meditation coach and an energy healer. She had been transparent with these coaches' as well in regards to what she was experiencing at home and that she had entered into an emotional relationship with someone outside of her marriage. She indicated that at times she even felt that she may be in love with this co-worker.

Her challenge was that she began to obsess and fantasize what a relationship with him would be like. He seemed to speak her language and she was attracted to his appearance, spontaneity and overall laid back persona. He was different than her husband and she felt like he possessed what her marriage was lacking. She maintained her physical boundary with him, but she definitely felt temptation at the same time.

As we began to explore her feelings, she also indicated that she had a tremendous amount of fear towards the idea of infidelity. She couldn't fathom the consequences of it due to the responsibility she felt she owed her husband, two children and even herself. She knew this, however she was also fearful that her marriage may not work out and that she might possibly lose an opportunity for a more meaningful relationship.

We also explored the feelings that she had for her colleague and why they were so intense. She felt that she had much more in common with him, and that he would be a better match than her husband was for her.

This was a key point in her transformation, as she began to examine the attachment she had to her colleague and the choices she had made based on her emotions. We visited her other relationship history with colleagues, partners, friends and her parents.

As we explored certain past experiences where she may have stepped out of her integral-self, she also noted times where the use of alcohol was an issue for her. This was not just in her marriage, but also friendships and family relationships. There were work functions and holidays where she noted she had become intoxicated, and arguments with co-workers or family members ensued. This was a recurring theme or a pattern for her in most of her experiences.

She also indicated that the relationship with her father had been very challenging to her, as he had left home when she was approximately five years old. She had not seen him since. Her mother had a series of other relationships that never lasted long. She also shared she had always longed for a father figure.

She discovered that she felt an emotional void in many of her current and previous relationships based on much of her childhood experiences. She decided to create resolve and explore this further, which gave her a wonderful sense of enlightenment. She had no idea that she had been harbouring so many emotional attachments for decades. This experience and her discovery brought her a sense of grace and gratitude.

This was also a great opportunity to explore fear and what her fears were really telling her about herself. Remember that fear is the barometer of the soul and tells us that we're off track. She came to understand that the fear associated with stepping out of her marriage had less to do with her husband and family and much more to do with her own emotions. It was in this instant moment of discovery that she began to see what integrity meant to her and why she had to make new choices. It was time to begin honouring her path and overcoming the temptations that lay before her.

She decided to commit further to her husband as she discovered that security was something that gave her much fulfillment. This included emotional and physical security. She recalled earlier times in the relationship with her husband when she had no interest in seeking this outside of her marriage. She also recalled the feeling of calmness and freedom during those times.

Although she was tempted by her colleague, as he appeared to be the complete opposite of her husband, she also recognized he had similarities to her father. She realized that part of the attraction was due to many of the experiences that she had encountered growing up. Some of these were her other attachments where she longed for security from a male figure. It was as if he was a fantasy that she could escape within like some of her other escapes. Of course most of these escape mechanisms were unhealthy in nature and included alcohol, workaholism and even people pleasing.

We explored how she would feel if her marriage dissolved, and she said it would not feel good to disrupt her family. She also indicated she could see that by building up her own self-worth and committing to her marriage, perhaps there was hope for deeper marital bliss.

We also explored the possibility that she may need to create a more concrete boundary with her co-worker as part of her own personal responsibility, to honour herself and resist temptation. Initially she disagreed with this possibility as she had feelings for him and did not want this relationship to end. She became angry, sad, jealous and frustrated at the idea of losing their friendship.

She continued to observe all of her emotions during the process of developing her integral-self. She also began to understand that although she loved her co-worker in many ways, her feelings were preventing her from making a rational decision with regards to her family.

It was in this discovery that she decided to step further into her own integrity and claim her own power by invoking personal responsibility. She realized she must create a healthy boundary with her colleague in order to maintain a professional friendship. If the boundary was crossed by either one of them, the working association would need to end on all levels.

She made a very clear choice, and subsequent declaration to her co-worker that although she valued their relationship and did not want to harm their working relationship, she could no longer see him in the same way that she had been. He understood this and asked how he could support her further. That was good enough for both of them, and she continued her own process.

We also created a ninety-day goal for her where alcohol was not to be involved. She committed to some minor adjustments to her diet and nutrition, along with a committed fitness plan.

Much like me, she did not understand this direction when we first began the process, however soon after she realized that it was quite beneficial and she was feeling much better about herself. Her husband even began to make the time to work out with her.

In just three months she noticed a greater feeling of pride about the choices she was making. She felt that she was living in integrity and noted major improvements at home. She and her colleague continue a responsible, professional relationship to this day.

This chapter is focusing on the continual process of staying aware in your own personal experience as tests and temptation can arise at any time. Honouring your own integral-path will be a guiding force to resist the temptations that present themselves to you.

As long as you commit to staying aware of your integral-self, and continue in this process of awareness and self-discovery, you will navigate with much more ease and flow. All of your outcomes will unfold more naturally and without the resistance that we often become far too familiar with.

Temptation can enter our experience in a ferocious manner. As we come to understand the aspects of addiction and attachment, these temptations can throw a curve ball into the integral experience if we do not exercise caution. There are many times that we feel like everything is moving along as it should be and then boom... something appears that takes us off our path or shakes up our world.

It doesn't matter what the temptations are. They will continue to present themselves in almost every experience we encounter. This is simply the way that our society works with the increasing advancements of technology and social media. We can find or have almost anything we think we want, and in very little time.

The key is to understand whether what we think we want aligns with the integral-self and if our choices are honourable and responsible in our own experience. A good question to pose to yourself on a consistent basis is as follows:

Am I reacting to what I think I want or am I responding to what my soul's true desire is?

One of the key ingredients to your success will be your ability to recognize these tests and make clear integrity-based decisions. We will continue to focus on your commitment to honour yourself and work on your integral purpose. We will discuss the Universal Law of Dharma and what integral purpose means to you.

Often times we have decisions to make that can leave us feeling fearful of the outcomes. Fear is an emotion and energy that I hope you will investigate and understand more for yourself. Understanding what fear actually is will be a great guiding system on your own path of integrity and honour.

Everyone is afraid of something. Our society programs us to believe that we should act a certain way, believe certain beliefs and live our lives in a way that society has determined acceptable. How daunting a task it is to maintain this high standard of living? I would venture to say it's actually impossible.

What I want you to understand about honour is that there is no wrong answer in what you define as your integral-self. Your experience is constantly changing and evolving. Your ability to make choices with your own free will may alter what integrity feels like and means to you. Our experience can change in an instant, and finding the opportunities in change will allow you to grow and evolve even further.

Purpose is something different. Discovering purpose and that which is your soul's true mission does not always happen overnight. What you will find is that by utilizing the tools and processes in this book to self-discover, determining purpose will also unfold more naturally as it works with your inner knowing.

Serving purpose can have a positive effect on your life but is often a challenging aspect to address as an individual. It's much easier to understand the external aspects of our lives and what they mean to us versus coming to understand our soul's true calling.

There is also a great difference between wants and needs and love and purpose. As you establish and honour your integral boundaries, you will be tested with temptations that challenge you. Understanding what truly serves your highest and most integral-self will allow you to honour your commitments and make mindful choices.

Remember that this process goes well beyond just understanding the words in a book or the processes I apply in my coaching programs. It requires both intention and action to honour your commitments to integrity. These are your intentions and your actions that you take to make them happen.

There will always be temptations and tests that creep up into our experiences, but how we navigate through them is what really matters. This will allow you to maintain a commitment to yourself with honour, and create more desirable outcomes time and time again. All of this will create more self-worth and a greater sense of pride, value and joy in each experience. You will also create experiences that have far less pain, agony and self-defeating outcomes.

When you are living a life of honour, the temptations that may appear in your life will not be considered as meaningful as perhaps they seemed in the past. Yes, you will want to be aware of them, however the impact these temptations have will not be as powerful as you will no longer consider them as so. This is one of the main reasons to focus on discovering your purpose in life and honouring that purpose day in and day out.

When we do not have clarity or a defined purpose, this is where irrational choices can produce unhealthy outcomes. This is why applying this work is ever so important to your personal and spiritual growth. When you view life with this perspective, and honour your purpose in spite of your fears, you will begin to find ways to create more meaningful experiences than ever before.

It is a misunderstanding of fear that causes the majority of the population to continually make the same choices over and over again. The feeling of fear often paralyzes us, or allows us to believe that we are not supposed to experience exceptional lives. It can prevent us from taking healthy risks and chances that may create outcomes beyond our wildest desires. This feeling may also prevent us from walking and honouring our true life path.

It is the misunderstanding of fear that keeps us tuned into low self-worth because we are often intimidated by the thought that something better could actually be happening in our experience. My goal for you is that you shift your perspective on fear. Understanding the emotion of fear is a gift.

Fear allows you to recognize and navigate the path of honour and temptation. When we find ourselves frightened, there is so much discovery and opportunity that most of us don't realize. Most of us don't realize that in our ordinary day-to-day lives, every bit of fear or discord is really just an opportunity to grow and evolve.

The energy that exists around fear will have a direct impact on your emotions and allow you to remain aware of your honour and responsibility. It will allow you to understand honouring your purpose, and the choices you must make in order to do so. Understanding and learning about fear is a good thing.

There are choices and decisions to make all of the time, and this applies to every aspect of your life. If you have created experiences that were out of integrity, such as an affair or some other form of breaking trust, then you will have the choice to make new choices to try and heal your existing relationship or yourself for future relationships. You will also have a choice to end that relationship if you feel that a more positive outcome exists in leaving.

What I ask that you pay close attention to here is the fear-based energy associated with honour, purpose and temptation. It is a guiding system to make healthy and responsible choices for each. It will also allow you to consult your own guidance system, which is your intuition.

If you are considering a relationship that exists outside of your current one, then you will want to recognize and work with the Universal Law of Cause and Effect further to understand that the choice you are considering will have a definite consequence. Are you prepared to accept the consequence, or are you fearful of the ramifications your choices may include?

If you have been betrayed, wronged, hurt or misled, then perhaps you get to decide if you want to heal yourself and the relationship that you are currently in. Perhaps you will decide if you want to leave the relationship to experience something different. Are you fearful of the opinions of others in regards to your relationship or are you deciding to discover and honour your own desires and purpose?

Again there are no wrong answers here, whatsoever. All that I ask is that you consider whether you are making a decision that feels good to you and aligns to your integral-self or if you are making a decision based on fear and the opinions of others. You alone get to define your honourable and most integral-self.

Are you resisting the decision to make changes in your life because you are fearful of the outcome? Are you allowing yourself to make a decision with a full knowing that you will support your highest self and receive the outcomes you desire? Are your associations having an impact on the decisions that you are making? Is it time to find and discover new associations? Is there fear associated with any of your choices to change?

You might have noted that I'm asking you a lot of questions in this chapter. You've read this far and are continuing to do the work, so I know that you're committed. What I want you to commit further to is discovering and honouring your own path. I want you to recognize your own gifts, passions and desires in regards to your own integral-self. It is here you will begin to engage your life's purpose.

Purpose can be anything for anyone as we all have one, which I'll explain at the end of this chapter. However, ask yourself what purpose you want to serve. Is it family, charity, leadership or contribution to other human beings? Could it be something else that truly fulfills you? Ask yourself if the decisions you are making are in alignment with that purpose.

In my own life, I assure you that I am constantly facing decisions I need to make in regards to temptation. The business I'm in provides a constant stream of new people to meet every day and chances to network in different settings. There are endless opportunities to revert to my previous self should I give way to the many temptations that cross my path.

I must maintain an awareness and level of personal responsibility to ensure I commit to integrity. Honouring my path includes my own temptations with people, places and circumstances at all times.

In the most authentic way possible, I have also come to recognize that I must continue to pose questions about my integral-self and discover and embrace change. I allow myself to feel fear when it arises and navigate my emotions accordingly. This allows me to make better choices, and it will work the same for you.

I do this by keeping committed to a process of staying in integrity and honouring my own path. I apply fitness and nutrition, personal or spiritual development, rituals, meditation and a continual process of learning from associations that focus on purposeful and integrity-based contribution.

This has allowed me to see that I wanted to share this knowledge with others. After years and years, I found that the passion I had in writing, coaching and speaking to people who faced challenges similar to my own created purpose and true meaning for me.

Whether I was writing a book, on a stage, or working with a committed client to facilitate growth and change, I knew that I was truly experiencing what my soul desired to do. There was no person, circumstance or external experience that would bring me as much joy and passion as the ability to contribute to others in this way.

The aspects of myself I had discovered would always be present including addictive tendencies, attachment issues, escape, and the experience of emotions that didn't serve my highest good. What I found was that when I stayed in my purpose and honoured my own path, I was able to navigate through these experiences and treat them as opportunities rather than road blocks.

Discovering purpose was something that allowed me to experience one of the greatest gifts and joys: reverence for life.

You can too.

The Universal Law of Dharma and Purpose

Everything in its entirety has a purpose on this planet. This is not limited to the people, places and things that we experience in day-to-day life, and the importance of this law is that it also applies to you.

All of the energy that exists around us serves a purpose in some way, shape or form. This includes physical and spiritual energy. Remember that everything is energy.

We can easily understand the purpose of our physical surroundings. Human beings, on the other hand, have a much more challenging time determining purpose due to the choices that we make in our own individual experiences and internal minds.

Often we forget that all things exist for a reason, including our own energy. Often the programming and experiences we've had in the past tell us what's good or bad versus our own internal knowledge.

Purpose can include our careers, volunteer work, charitable organizations we care about and our families. It can also be a contribution to humanity. Ultimately, purpose can be anything at all.

We are constantly reminded by outward experiences that we exist, however purpose allows us to align with our inner knowing and enjoy both spiritual and physical evolution together.

I want you to discover what your true integral-self feels like and eliminate the fears associated with living that life. You have been given a purpose and it is truly yours to discover.

Once you do discover purpose, you will begin to flow more freely, allowing all of your experiences to bring you reverence for life.

Often you will not see the results immediately, but I assure you that they will come to fruition. You will discover more meaning in your relationships with friends and loved ones, and will notice many of the circumstances that do not serve your integral-self will become insignificant. Often you will begin to enjoy some of the pure magic of the Universe, with signs and signals such as synchronicity to continually guide you on your path.

You will take joy in, more than ever before, because understanding and working in purpose will create a fulfillment that you have yet to experience.

You will move more fluidly in all of your positive experiences and align yourself to your soul's true desires, bringing an abundance of experiences into your existence.

CHAPTER 10 EXERCISES:

Discovering your soul's true purpose will allow you to work more effectively and efficiently in every area you desire growth in. Consider the following exercises to determine what might challenge your intentions, so you can see the path through any obstacles that stand in your way.

1. What are some temptations that continue to present themselves in your life?
2. What emotions do you feel when these temptations arise?
3. What are five things that you are proud of yourself for?
4. In what ways do you honour yourself on a regular and consistent basis?
5. What does purpose mean to you?
6. What intentions and actions are you taking to serve your life's purpose? Take the time to answer these exercises in your Integrity Vow Workbook.

Trust and Faith

> "I have faith in the universe, for it is rational. Law
> underlies each happening. And I have faith in my
> purpose here on earth. I have faith in my intuition,
> the language of my consciousness, but I have no
> faith in the speculation about Heaven and Hell.
> I'm concerned with this time - here and now."

> -ALBERT EINSTEIN

I RECEIVED A FRANTIC CALL from one of my coaching clients early on a Wednesday morning. This wasn't his usual appointment time and I could tell he was suffering. He was a young man in the insurance business who originally entered my program seeking to create a coaching program for his respective industry.

I could hear that he was crying over the phone, but he got right to the point of the call. "Ryan, I don't know what to do and I need you to fix my marriage." He was sobbing hysterically and had lost faith that things were going to be okay. His wife and he had been experiencing challenges in their relationship for quite some time.

Marriage counselling is not the work that I do, however people often seek marital advice from me. From my perspective marriage is an outer experience, while the process I facilitate is inward in nature. The clients I work with who desire growth and change can focus on all aspects of their personal experience, which then transfers to their outside world. This leads to new discoveries and will determine appropriate steps to reveal their own integral-selves.

There is no possible way for me to show anyone how to remain married forever. I say this, as although our intentions may be good, anything can happen at any time. Even in my own marriage there was not an outcome that I was attached to as the winds of change are always blowing. We never know what the Universe is going to serve up next. My hope is that those I work with learn to have faith in the process and begin to trust the decisions that they make.

Instead we commit to a process in which I facilitate account-ability, looking at their inward world versus all of the circumstances relating to their outside world. There is nothing about the outside world we can actually control, as control is nothing but an illusion anyway. One of my mentors phrased it well: if we want power, we must surrender control. In my own terms, I believe we must have faith in the way that the Universe works and trust in ourselves to continue on our individual paths accordingly. This is not always easy, however fear and mistrust are not ideal alternatives.

This chapter places an emphasis on having faith in all of our experiences whether they are practical, tactical or spiritual in nature. Every single choice that we ever make will lead to an outcome of some kind or another. What choices are you still unclear about? What out-comes are you seeking that may require a little more faith and a little less stress? Journal these answers in your Integrity Vow Workbook.

Faith can be defined as having complete trust or confidence in something or someone. My hope for you is that you begin to have complete trust and confidence in yourself as well.

Everything is showing up exactly as it is supposed to, based on the vibration that you are offering, and we must trust in the process rather than the end result. The Universal Law of Pure Potential is our primary focus in this chapter, which indicates that everything and everyone has infinite possibilities. The possibilities you may want to experience will still require you to take specific forms of action.

During my client's call he went on to share that he and his wife had been having marital issues for quite some time, and although I intuitively anticipated this it was not a normal topic of our discussions. He had not been fully transparent prior to this call.

His marriage had been in a downward spiral for several years and he was fairly certain it was going to end. Fighting, physical and verbal abuse, infidelity, substance abuse and financial challenges were the tip of the iceberg. They had a young son who he cherished beyond belief. The challenge was that he felt his marriage wasn't providing him with the happiness he desired in life. His perspective was that this unhappiness was causing all of his other problems.

I challenged his perspective on this.

They had separated, and during that time he began a brief affair with another woman. He and his wife later had discussions about reconciling and began marriage counselling in order to try to heal the marriage. Their intention was to create some unity and build new strategies for working through their marital issues.

In their last counselling session, before my client called me, his wife asked him if he had been with anyone romantically during their separation. He was truthful with her, as he felt that sharing the information would be the best thing to do, so he explained that he had seen a woman and had sex with her.

Upon hearing this information his wife became notably upset, left the meeting, and filed for a divorce the following day. She was absolutely devastated and appalled that he had said he was working on himself and yet he had been seeing another woman. He pleaded with her to reconsider, and was adamant that the relationship with the other woman was temporary and completely over.

His wife was unwavering in her decision, and indicated she found the exact clarity she was seeking in regards to the decisions surrounding their marriage.

My client was devastated and in an overwhelming emotional state. He began to blame his wife and himself for creating such a poor outcome and he couldn't fathom that telling the truth about his relationship could have resulted in a divorce. He appeared to have lost faith in everything, although I believe he had developed a certain level of mistrust in himself as well. It was time to examine himself rather than the situation.

We immediately moved into a place of him looking at aspects of personal responsibility. It was crucial that he allowed himself to feel all of the emotions he was experiencing. As he did this he began to develop an understanding of the choices that he made leading up to getting married and right up to the present time. Very quickly the negative charge lessened in his tone and he began to think rationally.

We also discussed the aspects of him in regards to what he defined as integrity. This was different than the emotional turmoil that he was experiencing. He was very attached and focused on what everyone in his life, including his wife and child, would think about a divorce.

Finally, I posed the question to him: "Deep down in the pit of your soul, do you feel that your wife complements the happiness, freedom and joy that you desire and deserve?"

It took less than ten seconds for him to answer "no." He had gotten very clear on what his integral-self looked like long before that conversation. It was in this moment, however, that he allowed himself to feel it. In the past he was so focused on the outcome that he wasn't allowing himself to realize the opportunity that existed in this area of his life.

We discussed his divorce as a great opportunity for him to discover more about himself and serve his purpose, which he defined as being a better father and continuing with his motivational speaking career. He began to see this as an opportunity, and completed the divorce with much more integrity than he would have had he not been willing to look within.

As we continued to coach together over the course of a year, he managed to create new habits and patterns that began to serve him. His rituals included journaling, meditation and a commitment to running five times per week.

He took responsibility for his workaholism and despite the co-parenting relationship that was created for his son, he became much more present as a father. He also began to take pride in some of the parental duties that he had not been accustomed to doing, which gave him faith in developing his feminine energy further. This began to allow him to trust more of his choices, which led to healthier outcomes and a trust in himself he had never experienced before.

Towards the end of the year he began dating again and indicated his relationship with his new girlfriend appeared to be much more suitable than any relationship he had previously experienced.

Many of the people I know question why I get up so early in the morning. Typically I wake up at 4:00 a.m. to start my day. I begin my day with gratitude, writing, meditation and a workout. I realize this may sound extreme to some and not so much to others.

For years I didn't sleep well, as I was pretty restless and seemingly troubled with my own internal struggles. I would question everything that was happening to me at all times rather than exploring how I created each experience. I would go to bed late and spend the night tossing and turning with all of the thoughts that stressed me out and the parts of me that were wreaking havoc on my soul. I had no trust in myself whatsoever.

Let's just say it was hard work being me. I was out of integrity, questioning everything I did and struggling with the darkness that lay within because I didn't know how to cope with being me or who I thought I was.

Does this feel familiar to you? Are you experiencing moments where you feel discord with yourself and are you struggling to fix something? It's time to have more faith and less resistance.

In this book, we've discussed the power of choice when it comes to staying in purpose as well as your own integrity. We've also examined how the Universal Laws can be understood further as powerful guidance to maintain your highest and most integral-self. What I want you to understand is that applying yourself to learning is one thing, however committing to the activity and taking action is much different. It is the actions you take on a daily basis that will yield you the results you desire.

You must also trust and have faith in this process.

The outcome that you may be seeking may or may not happen and that's okay. As long as you are staying in your highest and most integral-self, you will be presented with exactly what you need. My hope is that even at your most challenging times, you will begin to have faith in yourself and the Universe. I also hope that you will trust in the process and realize that you are exactly where you need to be in order to experience growth at any given time.

Your potential is completely unlimited to do whatever it is that your soul desires. It's a simple matter of understanding what that is, and we know this may take time too. Have faith that the answers you are seeking will continually reveal themselves to you, and having patience will be a great gift.

As you work with all of the Universal Laws and apply the appropriate action steps that I share with you in this book, your faith and trust will continue to yield more desirable outcomes in the outside world. The most profound impact however is the faith and trust you will develop for yourself.

Life doesn't just happen to us, rather we create and manifest all of our experiences. We have unlimited potential in any area that we focus on, and we can tap into this potential at any time. Your awareness and recognition of this will allow you to feel what you truly desire, and as we move into the next chapter we will look at the Law of Creation and the exact process to follow.

The key in the process is for you to trust and understand your own mission in life and what that means to you. Have faith that everything is always working out in your favour. Whether you want to be a musician, teacher, doctor, humanitarian or even watch countless hours of television, you have all the potential to do that which you desire.

I also want you to remember that this is a process and it's an ongoing commitment to maintain integrity, whatever that means to you. This chapter focuses on trusting the choices you make on an ongoing basis and trusting yourself with your decisions and having faith that everything will unfold as it should.

The principles apply to finding ways to trust yourself in your relationships with anyone you allow to be part of your personal experience. Our relationships are constantly evolving and changing as well, so creating elements of trust are crucial to ensure they remain long lasting.

Many people feel that when trust is broken, the betrayer needs to create the trust required for the relationship to succeed. I challenge this notion because even if one partner steps out of integrity, the other must build trust in themselves and make their own choices as well.

In order to build trust we must increase not only trust in ourselves, we must also begin to trust others too. There is a great difference between trusting ourselves and allowing ourselves to trust others. We can never control the decisions or actions of other people. It is impossible and virtually challenges every Universal Law that exists.

If you've stepped out of integrity in a relationship then you must recognize that building trust and reconciliation can be a long healing process as well. You will need to utilize your new found integrity in many ways and be very intentional with your actions. The work that you do on the inside is what's going to give you a chance at creating what you want in your outside experiences. Please remember that it also takes two people to have a relationship, so try to have compassion for yourself and others throughout the process.

You must also have faith that your partner is willing to do similar work to regain trust in the relationship and themselves. Remember that you may have shaken his or her reality. You cannot control whether he or she will commit to the work, but it will require both parties to build trust in yourselves and together as part of the healing process. Both partners must take responsibility in the healing process and this can be quite challenging at times.

Many of my clients introduce my coaching strategies and principles as a discovery for their spouses too. Although sometimes resistant, those that commit to doing this work together often strengthen and heal their relationships in far less time than they expected. In order for it to work, however, they both must have faith in each other and trust in the process. Only then can the Universe deliver what they are seeking.

If you feel like you've been betrayed, then the work that you learn in this process will also provide you with possibilities. The potential of these possibilities is for your own self-discovery and decision making. Often we feel that we have a lack of clarity as to what decisions we should make.

This is common and your eventual decision can happen at any point in your life. Creating a process for healing and understanding yourself further is of utmost importance, regardless of any outcome.

I have clients who have been betrayed in infidelity, molestation by their own parents, and physical abuse, and the principle applies in each case. You have an unlimited potential to heal any part of yourself that is not quite whole by understanding yourself further and making amends with your past. Whether you commit to remaining in any relationship with someone you feel has betrayed you is entirely up to you, and nobody can tell you what to do in the matter. It is up to you to find your own integral-self and trust in your ongoing decision making.

I want you to have faith that the darkness you have experienced in the past can be transmuted to light through an understanding and application of the principles in this book. Revisiting the chapter on grace and gratitude repeatedly will provide great benefits to you.

When you begin to put more faith into this process, you will also open yourself up to other gifts and divine guidance. One of these gifts is often referred to as intuition.

Have you ever been thinking about someone and then all of a sudden you get a Facebook message from that person? Can you reflect on situations that your intuition felt that something wasn't quite right? Did you follow that internal guidance and act accordingly? Intuition is abundant within you, and a deeper understanding of yourself will enhance this and many of your other gifts.

If you are considering entering into an inappropriate relationship, then I highly recommend you commit to a process of self-discovery first. Remember that the Law of Cause and Effect will provide you with an outcome no matter what you decide to do. Tread lightly with this as often the outcomes can be severe and not what you originally anticipated. There is a great difference when we act on physical wants such as lust, versus spiritual needs such as love. It is your personal responsibility to know the difference and choose accordingly.

In any case, sometimes we have good intentions, are taking action, but remain ambivalent as to what the right thing to do is. Finding clarity in certain situations or relationships can be overwhelming and paralyzing. We want good things, but don't quite know what they are or how to get there.

You're not alone. There are over seven billion people on the planet and all of them have moments where they find themselves questioning what decision they should make about one of their life choices.

Whatever your choices are, you will create new outcomes. Each new outcome will serve as a new opportunity to grow spiritually. The discoveries you make in this book and in the work that you do on your own will serve you time and time again. This will apply to all of your decisions and allow you to grow and evolve more than ever before.

Just know that whatever choices you are making are going to serve you the way that they are meant to. Having faith in the idea that the Universe provides us with everything we need at every moment of our lives is what will assist you in feeling good about your decisions.

We are constantly evolving, adapting and changing in all of the ebb and flow of the Universe. The possibilities for change are endless.

Instead of struggling with every single decision you need to make in life, I ask that you stop worrying about the outcomes and simply commit to the process. Worrying is not going to serve you in any capacity other than to create more confusion and an ongoing sense of overwhelm. Trust and faith will do just the opposite when it comes to helping you cultivate confidence.

Also remember that worrying is essentially coming from a place of lack which offers a lower vibration. Abundant thinking will result in you offering a higher vibration. Recall that the Law of Attraction dictates that like attracts like energy.

It's time to move away from attaching to the results you desire and commit to the activity of having faith in the process of self-discovery and developing your highest form of the integral-self.

Everyone has a different program and plan that they may adhere to, however the principles remain the same. What is going to make you happy and what must happen in order for you to continue to not only discover that answer, but enjoy the process along the way?

Instead of working on myself and having faith in what the Universe had provided me with, I masked my unhappiness with different addictions to escape the pain I was experiencing. I wouldn't wish such suffering on anyone as to have so much ambivalence about whether to stay in or leave a relationship. When children are involved the pain and suffering are amplified and can create an internal struggle that is near crippling. We can create an attachment to a relationship outcome that becomes debilitating and unhealthy.

When I released myself from the outcome of my marriage, and when my wife did the same, we began to follow our own paths which allowed us to understand each other further. We both trusted in the work that we were doing and had faith that the journey would bring us to where we were meant to be, whether that was together or apart. I will always recognize her commitment to our children, her own personal growth and mine. She was the true fighter in our relationship.

I believe we recognized that anything can happen at any time and attaching to an outcome that states "forever" is the only option would be unreasonable and unrealistic.

It was the process and rituals that I learned and applied that allowed me to continue to self-discover. I stopped worrying about what others were doing or thinking. Instead I began to seek out positive experiences that would allow me to create the highest state of consciousness I could.

Just because we do this work does not mean that we are going to save a relationship, other than the one that we have with ourselves. It's impossible to determine what happens in any marriage and constantly focusing on that can drive someone insane.

What I'm certain of is that understanding what my own integrity meant to me and trusting in my own decisions allowed for a much better version of me to appear each and every day. A constant commitment to staying aware and having the faith that everything would unfold as it should allowed me to move into a place of flow, versus the turmoil I had experienced in the past.

If there is anything I can do in this world as a father, it would be to educate and build my children's awareness up as high as possible. I want them to learn what integrity means to them and how the Universe works sooner than later. This too is out of my control, however as a parent I will provide them with continual examples and choices to discover for themselves.

I have faith that they will experience less heartache, chaos and drama than I have had in my own life. I am certain that they will have more education and opportunities to self-discover and build their self-worth at a much earlier age.

Regardless of the outcomes in my marriage, I trust that my wife and I will always provide them with the very best support possible. We will continue to give them the process and tools to navigate through any of life's changing experiences as they are not immune to what the Universe will allow them to experience. Nobody is.

My wish for my boys is that they have trust in themselves in whatever they do, they trust those closest to them including me, and they have faith that everything will work out, understanding that they create their own reality.

I could never explain to them how horrible it was that I stepped out of integrity the way I did. They were so young and I simply wanted to trust in myself more while protecting them from my indiscretions.

This was really why I began the process of working on myself. No matter what the outcome of my marriage, I wanted to create a healthier version of me in order to be the very best father that I could for them.

Some day they will read this book and quite possibly learn something different about me that they did not realize. I have faith that they will see a man who wanted to make changes not only for himself, but because of an absolute unparalleled love of his children.

I trust in the Universe and that it will look after my children exactly the way that it should, and that it will help guide me as a father. Of course they too will be presented with their own challenges and will grow and evolve accordingly.

Instead of hoping for all of their best outcomes or the outcome of the relationship with my wife, I have faith that all is as it should be and everything works out. There is a great difference between hope and faith. My perspective on hope is that it is scarcity based, while faith is abundant in nature.

Others have asked me about my own journey and why I didn't leave my marriage when I thought that it was ending during my affair. I've also had people indicate that the damage I caused and the lack of integrity I showed towards my wife, children and myself would never be able to be healed. Everyone is entitled to their own opinion and perspective. This again is free will.

We were definitely taking a risk as far as losing more time in our lives if our marriage didn't work out, however we also both realized that something was holding us together rather than pushing us apart and away from one another. How long or if that would last was yet to be determined.

It is the same for many of my coaching clients and I am certain it is for you. Whether you decide to leave a relationship or reconcile one, you will need to become clear on what it is that you want in your own integral-path.

Your possibilities are endless and your unlimited potential is absolute. Many of my clients find a deep path of discovery that produces enlightenment on many levels. What they choose to do with that new discovery will also lead to new choices and outcomes.

I cannot speak for my wife and it would not be responsible to suggest that she stayed out of hope or faith. I am certain that these were the exact reasons why *I* decided to recommit to my marriage when I did and it was the most integral-path at the time.

I knew that there were parts that existed in me that wanted more out of life. I wanted to be a better husband, father, co-worker, and human being. I realized that I had so much work to do to make improvements but I had hoped that I could make some changes which would then impact my relationship at home.

My wife realized the same. We had spent so many years finding external circumstances to keep us busy and escaped from looking at ourselves. We had allowed our careers, parent roles, children's activities, associations and many other aspects of life to become priorities over our relationship together and the relationships we had with ourselves. We placed an emphasis on everything that existed outside of us rather than doing the personal work we discuss in this book.

I believe we both realized that there was potential to improve our relationship, however in actuality it was a journey to change ourselves. There would never be a firm answer as to whether our marriage would last or not. I was certain that the journey we both embarked on would benefit ourselves and all of our other experiences including those of our wonderful children.

The personal development work I do is ongoing and is definitely a part of tapping into my full potential. This work has allowed me to serve others, including my family and everyone I experience.

Your possibilities are endless as well, and as you continue to have faith in this process, trusting in the Universe and your integral-self, you too will experience the happiness and freedom you desire.

Universal Law of Pure Potential

Most people never really live up to their full potential or understand just how powerful this law actually is. It's important to recognize and understand as it can have an immediate impact on shifting your mindset.

There are no limits to what any of us can do in the life that we have been given. Let me say that again: your potential is completely unlimited.

Remember that everything is energy and aligning your energy with your intentions can be done at any time. There is no limit to the amount of energy you can direct.

If you recognize this, you will understand that there are infinite possibilities when it comes to directing your energy, and this is the same for everyone.

You must take personal responsibility when working with this law, as the only challenges you face in working with it are your self-limiting beliefs and habits.

The reason people often don't realize or truly work with this law is that they are uninformed, have low self-worth and self-defeating beliefs, or are not intentional with their actions.

It doesn't matter what your circumstances currently are. Miracles happen every day so consider that your opportunities are endless.

These opportunities are always present and waiting for you to tap into. This is your potential.

This is why it is so crucial to apply the process and action steps that you've learned in this book and maintain a commitment to them.

Your intentions, actions, and all of your worth depend on you remaining focused and committed to your potential. Sometimes we find short-term success but this is where we can also become most at risk for moving backwards.

My purpose is to continue to move you forward into your absolute highest potential and most integral-self.

CHAPTER 11 EXERCISES

As you've discovered in this chapter, the process I facilitate places a great emphasis on trust and faith. Consider these exercises to allow you to explore how you place faith in the Universe, other people and yourself.

1. When have you experienced times where your trust has been tested? This applies to yourself and others.
2. Can you recall instances where you sensed your intuition and trusted it or did not trust it? What were the results in both instances?
3. In what areas of your life would you like to have more faith? Journal your answers in your Integrity Vow Workbook.

Courage

"It takes courage to grow up and
become who you really are."

-E.E. CUMMINGS

"I WANT YOU TO PICTURE yourself in an empty white room. The only other person standing in the room with you is your wife."

Our marriage therapist had asked me to close my eyes and begin to visualize.

"I want you to walk up to her with compassion and look into her eyes. Thank her for the blessings that she has given you since the time that you have been together."

I thought of our children and what gifts they were and her support throughout my personal challenges and career.

"Tell her that you love her and that it has been an honour spending time with her. Thank her for the gift of being parents together."

When the therapist said this, I felt sadness come over me, as if I were mourning the loss of someone at a funeral.

"Look down at your hands and take your wedding ring off. Put it in your pocket and realize you won't be putting it back on. Look into your wife's eyes and thank her again. Now tell her you love her once more and say goodbye."

I felt one of the deepest emotions of grief as I visualized myself saying goodbye to her.

"Turn around and start slowly walking. You're worried about your children, but look back at your wife and picture them with her and know that they are okay. They look at you with love and know they will see you very soon. Turn back around and keep walking, only this time you're on an open road. Walk for a while noticing the open road. Eventually the road leads you to a doorway to enter, and once again you're in a white room, only this time there is a mirror. Walk up to the mirror and look at your reflection.

Ask yourself what you see in the mirror. Who is the man standing in front of you? How does he feel when he looks at himself? What does the man in the mirror say?"

I thought about this for a moment and as sadness and peace came over me all at once, I replied to the therapist,

"You did the right thing."

Have you ever experienced moments where, in order to do the right thing, it required courage with the highest expression of love possible?

Have you expressed your most integral-self by overcoming the fears associated with the opinions of others? Have you truly loved yourself enough to make the right decision for you? Could you find the courage to love others, such as your children, enough to make new choices?

If you are struggling with a secret you have been keeping, would it benefit you and those you cherish most to have the courage to expose yourself and surrender to the outcome? If you are in a challenging situation and have done enough work to gain clarity, can you accept that by making the courageous choice to change, you will transform your life?

Can you accept that nothing outside of you is in your control? Do you realize there is a divine guidance that is always available to you if you change your point of attraction and raise your own vibration?

This chapter focuses on the Law of Acceptance and the Law of Love, through courage. In stepping into our highest and most integral-self, it often requires courage to express what our soul's true desire is. It is here we find acceptance in all that is and understand that there is a divine guidance working for us, rather than against us.

We step further into integrity and express the highest form of it, which is the love of self and others. I believe this is also a place where we find courage to move beyond our deepest fears and suffering, and apply the Universal Law of Love. This is the highest form of manifestation. Remember that our energy is our point of attraction and unconditional love is the purest form of energy in the Universe.

This chapter is about courage, which can be defined as the ability to do something that frightens one or find strength in the face of pain and grief. In order for you to evolve to the most integral-self possible, you will need to tap into your inner courage.

My wife and I separated the day before Father's Day. There was a challenging few weeks leading up to that day and the emotions were running high. We weren't fighting, but we were very distant and I observed that I was even more distant than she was.

We had been seeing a couple's therapist for about a month, based on the recommendation of a colleague. We had identified that although we had healed much of our marriage and were doing our own personal work, we lacked a great deal of intimacy and had merely co-existed for many years.

We are both two highly committed parents despite doing things differently. We are both good human beings and had good intentions to continue working on our marriage as well.

I have to give my wife credit for her courage to work so hard on us time and time again despite everything that had happened over the course of our twelve-year marriage. Her commitment to our relationship was nothing short of remarkable. Her courage to try and heal our marriage after I betrayed it will always be considered one of the bravest acts I've experienced.

The weeks and months leading up to our separation, I found that most of my one-on-one coaching clients were having challenges in their relationships too. It took me into a deep place of centering and looking inwards at my own integral-self. I noticed that as I went through the discovery process with most of my clients, there was a great deal of discovery happening for me as well. I began to recognize some clear signals that, although I was acting in integrity within my marriage, my deep knowing about how I felt about the marriage was not in alignment with my integral-self.

I challenged some of the assignments that our therapist gave us as I felt that they were very external-based. They appeared to contradict much of the work I had been doing over the course of several years. They didn't align with Universal Laws or discovering integrity, but rather they were more about how to fulfill the needs of someone else. I felt that this was not possible and went against my own beliefs. We must change our inner world and love ourselves before we can realize changes in our outside world and receive love from others.

As we discussed my feelings, the therapist stopped me and told me that she felt I had checked out of the marriage. Right there and then she asked me a simple question: "If you want a divorce, what are you afraid of?"

In that moment I realized that I had surrendered and I was no longer afraid of expressing what my own integrity was telling me. My marriage had come to an end and I needed to find the courage to tell my wife. Over time, she too reflected that although she would have stayed longer, she acknowledged I made a courageous decision that was difficult for both of us.

I've never met a stronger or more courageous human being on the planet than my wife. She spent over a decade navigating through a marriage that was rooted in suffering and lacked integrity.

She continued to work on our relationship, despite my bouts with alcohol, temper, instances of verbal abuse and eventually the lack of personal integrity that led to my infidelity.

Her commitment to our children and to me during our entire relationship was unparalleled from a loving and trusting place, and the gifts that she gave to all of us were beyond belief. She did her very best to be an exceptional mother and wife at all times.

Her natural beauty, integrity, pureness and heart are assets that anyone would treasure in her. She is an exceptional woman and mother and I cannot give her enough credit for my experience with her.

The choice to divorce was the hardest decision I have ever made in my life and it took me years to come to terms with. I had struggled with the emotional turmoil, guilt of past experiences, and wondered what would unfold for our family if we separated. The thought of giving up or letting my children down in any way brought on intense, excruciating pain.

Everybody wants a happy ending, but I'm unsure that most people realize what happy actually means. Society paints a picture of what happy is supposed to be, but in reality we can only determine that for ourselves.

I suppose it's different for everyone when it comes to relationships. I can still recall very happy times with my wife when we first began dating. I would buy her flowers, introduce her to wonderful restaurants and constantly tell her how much I loved her.

She was expressive however not as expressive in our relationship as I had hoped, and I found that the more that I did this, the more I sought something in response from her. When I did not receive what I felt was fulfilling, I would escape, numb myself to the experience, or act out with negative words and emotions. Of course there is no justifying my actions or the lack of integrity I held in our relationship at the time.

I believe that much of my experience with her was one in which I expected something in exchange for all the love I was giving to her. The challenge was that we both expressed love differently and we never took the time to understand that. We were engaged after a year of dating, married with a house a year later, and proceeded to have our first of three children next.

My perspective is that we became very attached to outcomes quickly, which is also a form of control. We put pressure on ourselves to achieve certain things in our careers, home life and family without truly understanding each other. In my deepest truth I don't believe we had a true understanding of ourselves.

This is the challenge I find in the description of love. We consider unconditional love to be the highest and purest state of being. More often, however, our society programs us to love one another with a massive amount of conditions. When we place conditions on our love, we are fear-based and offering lower vibrational energy, versus unconditional love. Unconditional love is authentic and unlimited by conditions. It only offers a higher vibration and asks for nothing in return.

"If you do this, I will be happy." "If this happens, we will be happy." "If you don't do this, you don't really love me." All of these relate to external circumstances which have nothing to do with love, and everything to do with ego.

This false sense of love is the breeding ground for why so many marriages are unhealthy and challenged by an attachment to outcomes. We become so certain that we must have certain things, or play a certain part to adhere to society, that we never come close to understanding what love actually is.

We can sit in our relationships for years, and even decades, just getting by and co-existing. Often this will lead to more unhappiness, which can then bring out more of the negative aspects that exist in our partners or relationships. Eventually this negative cycle may breed the potential for more and more unhealthy choices.

An inappropriate relationship is often one that is loaded with conditions and manipulation of the self and others. We create drama and chaos which lower our vibration further. It becomes more and more challenging to attract positive experiences into our lives when we participate in an affair.

On the other hand, the person who is betrayed must look inside to determine if staying in a relationship and healing the self are going to create more self-love or not. If the answer is no, that person cannot possibly stay and commit to loving his or her partner. It goes against Universal Law.

Finally, those who are considering any relationship or circumstance that is out of integrity must consider how it will affect their own self-worth and those around them. Intuition can often give us that answer immediately, however courage is usually what is required to make the right choice.

Over the course of my marriage I did something that I truly regret, which was what I term as "throwing out the divorce card" frequently when we would argue. Although it may have been my intuition telling me early on in our marriage that this was the path that would unfold, creating insecurity for my wife was one of the most regretful things I have done.

I didn't realize it at the time, as I had no clarity about myself or what integrity was for me, so I was never truly aware to my wife's experiences. All of my actions were based on my own selfish needs, and despite trying to be a decent father, my integrity did not allow me to fulfill that as much as I had hoped.

When we agreed that the marriage was over, we were also faced with the fact that we would need to tell our children. This would prove to be the most painful experience of my life.

Our children were not expecting the news that Mommy and Daddy were separating. They didn't understand it. This will always be an image that haunts me until the day I die. We all cried together for a long time as the news sank in.

My wife and I love our children more than anything in the world, and we are absolutely committed to giving them that love, despite being apart. Within seventy-two hours of telling them the news, we found the courage to come together, create a full schedule for the children and sort out almost every financial detail required to work through the process of living apart. Of course there were challenges to navigate in the process and it wasn't perfect by any means.

We all want what is best for our children. It is so difficult to make these types of decisions when kids are involved because we fear that we are hurting our children. The most important advice I can give to someone who is ending a marriage where children are involved is to focus on your own vibration. Ensure that even when it is tough, you find the courage to raise your energy level and show unconditional love for your children, your former spouse and yourself.

It sounds cliché, however if I had known prior to stepping out of my marriage what I know now, I would have applied my own teaching to the fullest degree. I would have known what the energy of an affair offered me and what I was offering in return. I would have examined the lack of self-love I was exhibiting which transferred over to my family. Regardless of my marital outcome, the experience would have been different if I remained in integrity.

Consider your vibration and what you are truly offering if you are on the verge of making a decision to act outside of your own integrity vow. My hope is that a strong consideration of this will lead you to an integral-choice.

It is interesting to reflect on this as so many of my coaching clients discuss the turmoil and chaos that surrounds their relationships.

It always intrigues me to watch two human beings who completely loved each other at one point become hateful and resentful. The way that people can turn on each other and the impact it has on children can be devastating. It is also Karmic, which is why I wanted to ensure we dissolved our marriage with integrity.

Your choice is to apply the information and action steps found in this book to what you desire change and growth in. It doesn't have to be a relationship with someone else all of the time. Often it is the choices to make changes for you.

Are you finally ready to love yourself fully in order to love others and fall in love with many of the experiences and opportunities that are available to you?

Are you prepared to be courageous and take action to make the necessary changes that you know will serve your highest and most integral-self?

Perhaps you'd like the courage to leave a relationship where someone has betrayed or misled you. Perhaps you need to share your story with someone before you create an outcome that you know will not serve you. Perhaps you need to ask for help from someone else in order to heal the relationship with yourself and others.

In any case, you will need courage. You will need to have the courage to love yourself enough to make a decision and detach from the outcome associated with that choice. You will need the courage to trust in the divine guidance that the Universe offers you. You must understand that there is something much bigger than you that will serve you in creating the experiences you desire. The Universe will provide you with everything you need, and more love for yourself and others, if you have the courage to do the work.

One of my coaching clients signed up for a twelve-week program to discuss how to create more real estate business. She was resistant to investigating her own time management process, choices, boundaries or looking at what an integrity-based program could help her accomplish. It was as if anything we discussed was understood and yet quickly dismissed.

She was one of my friendliest clients and worked with me for close to a year. I often questioned why she continued to stay with the program, as often she would not commit to the activities we discussed, but rather she appeared grateful for the time we spent together.

Finally, after close to a year of working together, I stopped her mid-call and told her that I was going to send her money back. I explained that we could talk and talk, however, unless she wanted to get transparent about what was really happening in her life, she would not get the results she was seeking. I have empathy for all of my clients, but I am in the results business, and it was time to call her out.

It took courage to be this direct with her as she was a wonderful soft-spoken lady who was in her early sixties. My hope was that she would mirror my tact and get more transparent about what was going on in her experience.

Originally I thought she was lonely and really just wanted someone to speak with regularly to clear her mind. During the time of our coaching, she had referenced a relationship that she had left a couple of years earlier. We applied much of the process to her resentment for her ex-boyfriend and worked through many of the principles you've read in this book. This included addressing personal responsibility, integrity, detachment, low self-worth and resistance.

Her entire energy changed over the time we worked together, but often my intuition advised me that something had not come to completion or been resolved. When I called her out on this, she went silent for about five minutes. It was the longest pause I've ever had on a coaching call, and it felt like an hour.

Suddenly she broke down in tears. She explained to me that she was an alcoholic and hadn't recognized it. She was drinking six to ten glasses of wine a night and functioning through the day. Nobody knew about it besides her and the cashier at the liquor store. She also indicated that her ex-boyfriend had turned her onto cocaine and her usage was increasing.

There is nothing more courageous then asking for help when you need it and bringing forth your most authentic self. It requires transparency, vulnerability and integrity. It is also the place where great transformation can occur.

I paused with my client and asked her one question: "Do you love yourself enough to get some help?" She immediately responded yes and we began the integrity process together. We also found other resources that would serve her well on her path to recovery. I'm pleased to say that she has been sober since then with no relapses.

What changes do you desire, whether they are big or small, that will allow you to love yourself and others more? What areas of growth are you seeking that will give you the ultimate experience you've been searching for and a newfound reverence for life? My coaching client showed courage by becoming transparent and asking for help. What area of life do you need to exercise courage in?

If you apply the process in this book you are going to discover just that. You will realize that every part of your integral-self is healthy and ready if you have the courage to love yourself just a little bit more. Happiness and freedom are waiting for you on the other side of understanding fear.

It's time to make a choice.

There are stories of the courageous throughout history. We don't need to look very far to see them.

Nelson Mandela had the courage to fight against the unjust system of the apartheid and was sentenced to twenty years in prison.

The Dalai Lama led a non-violent movement against Chinese rule in Tibet.

Muhammad Ali refused to fight in the Vietnam War despite threats of jail sentencing.

Story after story exists regarding those who have had to seek courage, and in many cases, challenge the norms of society. There are so many of these stories of people that reached deep within themselves to stand up for what they believed in and make a difference.

So why don't we find the courage to stand up for ourselves and finally love ourselves at the highest level possible? Why do we put conditions on the love of self?

I referenced it earlier, but change doesn't happen over time. Circumstances do. Change happens in the instant that you make a choice to do something different with your life. Change happens immediately when you make that choice because you instantly start moving in another direction.

Sometimes it takes courage to make big decisions. It takes courage to make choices that you're scared about. It can be tough to stand on your own and do what you know is best for you. It requires the love of self and the understanding that everything works in perfect harmony with the Law of Attraction. When you maintain acceptance, integrity and alignment, you will always be protected.

What is getting in the way of your integrity? Where might you need to find courage in any particular experience right now? What is getting in the way of loving yourself the right way and knowing what that will attract into your life? When will you have the courage to accept certain things and challenge others? When will you accept yourself and challenge yourself all in one?

When is it going to be time to take a stand for yourself and surrender to your own path of least resistance? If you tune into your own divine guidance, everything will unfold with more ease.

I promise you it will.

Universal Law of Acceptance

The Universal Law of Acceptance can be a great gift to understand further. In utilizing this law, we come to understand that there is a greater power than just us as individuals. I refer to this as Divine Guidance.

We cannot make big decisions or changes until we learn that we must accept ourselves for all that we are. We must also accept those we wish to have relationships with as all that they are. Finally we must accept that the Universe is all that it is and that it is more powerful than we can possibly imagine.

When we find acceptance in all of our circumstances, we begin the surrendering process. We surrender to ourselves, our circumstances and the Universe. As we surrender, we can become very present and begin to heal the pain that is buried deep within our souls. It is when we feel this pain and embrace it, rather than resisting it, that we heal. This too allows us to heal others.

Acceptance is not always easy as the ebb and flow of the Universe does not always appear to be in alignment with the way that we think life is supposed to be. Those that work well with this law will treat every situation they encounter as an opportunity to evolve spiritually.

This requires courage to understand others and the integral-self. It requires compassion and empathy for others and the self. It also requires trust and faith that everything is working for us versus against us.

Acceptance allows us to avoid denial and step forward into our integral-path. It also allows us to utilize our spiritual gifts such as intuition to find further clarity with relationships or other experiences. When we find this clarity, it allows us to make new choices and decisions.

The Universal Law of Love

This law indicates that love is universal energy in its purest form or state. This is my favourite law as I believe it to be the most powerful of all Universal Laws.

This is the law I reference in regards to our highest state of being: unconditional love for others and ourselves. There is no other state that will allow us to create more desirable outcomes.

You can begin to invoke this law with practices such as meditation and energy awareness, and by paying attention to your heart chakra.

Chakra work is among my favourites and a field of energy study that I recommend you explore. Consider local Reiki practitioners to get started on understanding chakras and how you can redirect your energy at any time.

When you apply unconditional love to yourself and others, you offer a vibration that is pure and in harmony with the Universe. Finding a place of awareness will also further develop your most integral-self.

One thing you will want to consider is that you must focus on receiving pure love as well. Any love that is attached to conditions is fear-based and will not manifest that which you desire. Often this can be challenging to recognize, but over time and with practice you will.

Love is the purest state of being and not an action. The more you recognize this and apply the process of self-love, the more your outer world will shift to your ideal experience.

CHAPTER 12 EXERCISES

Utilize these exercises to explore where courage and love may be needed in your life. Understand and appreciate yourself further as you continue to engage your authenticity.

1. Write down five times in your life when you've exercised courage and the outcome was favourable.
2. Where in your life do you need to grant acceptance?
3. What choices would you like to make, but are having a hard time finding the courage to do so?
4. List ten things that you love about yourself.
5. When you think of the word love, do you consider it conditional or unconditional? Journal your answers in the Integrity Vow Workbook.

CHAPTER 13
Creation and Manifestation

"Creativity is the state of consciousness in which
you enter into the treasury of your innermost being
and bring the beauty into manifestation".

-Torkom Saraydarian

What experiences are you creating as you move forward onto your own integral-path?

Are you crystal clear on your desired outcomes and do you have the necessary vision to ensure you remain focused?

The most highly recognized and commercialized Universal Law is the Law of Attraction. There are hundreds of books indicating that the power of our thoughts dictate our reality. Countless authors have created work that supports this law's premise that like energy attracts like energy.

In my own life I am certain of this and continue to experience the art of manifestation by directing my thoughts to create my reality and all of my experiences.

This chapter discusses manifestation and the power of the mind as it applies to creating preferred experiences. We place an emphasis on manifestation and revisit the Universal Law of Attraction and examine the Law of Creation.

Everybody these days seems to know the "secret" in theory. The process of manifestation is laid out clearly for us, yet how many people are actually creating what they truly desire? There are millions of people reading the books, but how many are actually understanding manifestation and truly seeing the results?

I believe much of the information available fails people in truly teaching the process of creation. Until we dig deeper in identifying and healing our integral-selves, we commonly create the opposite of what we desire. As we've discussed earlier, some of the experiences that we create are also unhealthy and even chaotic.

If you were to look at your own overall experience in current space and time, what would you say is being created? Is life happening to you or are you using your emotions, awareness of integrity, rituals and this process to create more desirable outcomes?

We've all had the perfect picture painted, from school or the media, of what a perfect family and home with a "white picket fence" looks like. We are shown what success looks like in terms of money and material items. The picture of happiness is often instilled into us by a societal definition of what happiness is and how relationships are supposed to be.

I challenge the notion that the majority of people on the planet truly desire this. The international divorce rate would clearly indicate that many of those who pursue this image of what society deems successful are not truly living in their own integrity, and seldom achieve the results.

Domestication is rewarded while freedom to express the highest and most integral version of self is often ridiculed or punished.

I want to be clear that I am not an advocate for divorce by any means. I am not pro-marriage by any means either. It took me over ten years to determine that my marriage was going to end in a divorce. Finding my own integral-self allowed me to discover the best path moving forward and will continue to create new opportunities, whatever they may be.

In all that is possible, what I share is that you have an opportunity to manifest and create whatever you desire. You can apply manifestation to every single experience in your life including finance, relationships, love, health, and your career. As we discussed earlier, the Universal Law of Potential indicates that your potential is unlimited. I believe when you move away from your fears and into your integrity, you will then discover what you truly want to manifest.

We are only limited by our own beliefs. This is why the integrity process is so important to work through and continue to examine. The programming we often have instilled in early childhood keeps us from discovering what we truly want, let alone creating it. We are told that we are not good enough, smart enough, or capable enough to manifest our dreams.

We are given and shown examples of poor role models who are facing their own challenges and their own unhealthy outcomes. This can be parents, peers and authority figures. I believe that most humans do not truly follow their dreams to the highest capacity possible. Something gets in the way, and more often than not it is ourselves.

The coaching I do places a focus on what is often referenced as the grand trilogy: Body, Mind and Spirit. I believe my responsibility is to pass on and contribute what I have learned. Much of it was passed on to me by my own mentors and guides, to help me shape and create a higher version of myself.

Most of my coaching clients enter my program because they want to create more business. More often than not they quickly realize that until they gain clarity, step into integrity, and understand themselves and their soul's true desires, there is no amount of business that will satisfy them. It is when they discover their own integrity that they can begin to manifest their soul's true vision.

Not all of my clients believe in the manifestation or creative process when they first begin. They often resist and indicate that they would prefer to keep our coaching sessions business-related.

I always accept this, as we must be ready to allow ourselves to receive, prior to manifestation. I learned early on in my own experience that when the student is ready, the teacher will appear.

More often than not, my clients tend to get more and more transparent about the life they are experiencing. They often determine that business is also an escape from the painful experience of looking at themselves and their other life experiences. In order to create positive outcomes through manifestation, it requires a heightened state of awareness of the self.

When I first made the choice that my marriage was ending I felt a mix of emotions, which is natural for such a massive life change. I could be quite confident and brimming with the excitement of new opportunities. I could also be sad and resentful, feeling guilty, hurt and even depressed at times. It was a literal roller coaster of emotions day in and day out.

My highest and most integral-self requires a strong nurturing of the body. It is my conscious awareness that allows me to experience that which I desire when it comes to creating the healthiest version of me.

What I noticed early on in my separation was that I was stepping backwards at times. I caution anyone who is going through this type of life change to really focus on staying in a place of awareness. This will enhance your ability to create healthier experiences.

I mentioned earlier that I have spent time working on my own addictive challenges, and recognize the impact of alcohol on my vibration and overall experiences.

Although alcohol had been long removed as a negative part of my lifestyle, I experimented with the occasional glass of wine at night. I did this primarily when my wife was with our children and I was out of the house in the initial part of our separation.

I began to notice some of the darker parts of me that were beginning to surface again. I felt a lower vibration during the day even if I had only had one drink. This is because alcohol was so foreign to my body, and therefore the effects were suddenly more severe.

This did not result in the experiences that I hoped to create, which was ultimately an amicable divorce from my wife, and bringing the best version of myself to our children.

Instead, my choice to experiment with alcohol brought forth more depression and mood swings, and additional tension at home with my wife as we navigated our separation. I noticed that my energy was not as healthy when it came to my children, work or other friendships and I decided to stay committed to my healthier path.

The path to your most integral-self is one of awareness and commitment. In order to create and manifest the experiences that resonate with your soul, I recommend that you commit to becoming the healthiest version of yourself possible.

This applies to any relationships. If you wish to create new outcomes with your previous partner, then there will be a commitment to creating a better version of you.

If you have been involved in an inappropriate relationship and you are hoping to heal your existing relationship, creating a more integral and healthy path will be of utmost importance here also.

Perhaps you have been on the other end of the spectrum and someone has misled or betrayed you. Whether you decide to recommit to the relationship or leave to create new opportunities, you will want to bring your highest and most integral-self to that situation too.

Manifestation is not only about relationships. Whatever the outcome you desire, remember that everything is energy. Your goal is to strive for the highest energetic vibration you can. This is the love of self. Until you love yourself fully and completely, or at least commit to the path of self-love and integrity, often your manifestations will be similar to those of past manifestations. Perhaps they will not be exactly the same, but often they will be similar and unhealthy, and you will repeat past patterns.

This is a good time to pause and consider what's currently happening in your own experience. You're continuing to discover what your integrity means to you and dissolve what it does not mean. You desire more growth, change and spiritual evolution, I'm sure. Do you have a crystal clear vision of what that looks like for you? Are there any circumstances that may possibly get in the way of that crystal clear vision you hold? Take a moment and journal your answers in the Integrity Vow Workbook.

There are great answers in your own examining and exploration that will aid you in manifesting exactly what you truly want.

Consider whether or not many of your manifestations are similar to those from the past and whether they have a recurring theme of positivity or negativity. Consider whether your energy and overall vibration have been similar as well.

Often we can recognize that what we create has a familiarity to it. What we don't understand is why the creations continue when we don't desire them. All of the chapters and work on attachment, addiction and previous programming will support you in uncovering this further.

This is also where I've referenced reflecting and considering your current manifestations and creations. Reflect by considering previous experiences that were similar. Understanding and determining what programmed beliefs you have will guide you in realizing why your manifestations have often taken place. Again this can be challenging and painful at times, but your unconscious mind holds secrets and wonderful gifts if you allow yourself to experience them.

This is where I would challenge many of the commercial works on Law of Attraction or manifestation. The principles of visualization and holding thoughts about that which you desire are crucial, but that is only part of the process and also only of the conscious mind. This is why many people fail in the process when they first set out to manifest.

Remember that the conscious mind thinks while the unconscious mind acts. A mentor once taught me this principle and it holds true as a great reflection in awareness.

When you do a deep and personal examination of the painful parts of your past, it will bring to the surface what you may not have realized before this process. These are parts of you that you must discover to allow your inner light to shine, then and only then can you find alignment with what you wish to manifest and your integral-self.

A client came into my program and had a wonderful spiritual background. She meditated daily, went on spiritual retreats and had an incredibly positive outlook on life. She followed along with the Universal Law of Attraction and even believed that she manifested her son's recovery from a severe illness.

What we began to recognize during our coaching together was that although she had a great positive outlook, often times she could find herself in conflict with colleagues. She didn't know why she continued to create these experiences and referenced that she always held positive thoughts for even the most difficult and challenging of people.

She had indicated that she had been having these experiences for over ten years in her profession and the frequency of these disputes was often.

Remember that the Law of Attraction shows us that like energy attracts like energy. We do not attract what we want, however we attract what we are.

It was important for my client to recognize that although she maintained great intentions, there was something inside of her that she had not recognized as part of herself. I asked her to visit other experiences where she had become upset, angry and confrontational.

She recognized that through most of her life including her past relationships, schooling and even in early childhood, these experiences were familiar.

She also identified that she grew up as a middle child and most of her childhood memories involved arguing or fighting with her younger brother and older sister. She indicated that she had a strong desire to always prove herself or be right. When I asked her about her feelings towards her parents and siblings regarding these arguments, she expressed very little compassion towards them and instead seemed resentful.

The benefit of this discovery was that we were able to identify one of the traits in her that she had not previously recognized. As she began to discover what was buried deep in her unconscious mind, she decided that she wanted to make some changes.

These changes included more self-discovery, finding compassion for others and herself, along with a process to create self-awareness and love for all of her experiences.

Months later when we discussed her work and how she rated the interaction she had with colleagues, she noted great improvement. She felt that she had maintained a much higher level of personal responsibility and integrity in all of her business encounters. She also noted similar improvements in her other experiences.

What experiences from your past may be showing up in your daily creations and manifestations for you?

My hope is that you continue to self-discover using this principle of personal responsibility to the best of your ability. I assure you it will have a dramatic effect on what you wish to create in your life.

In order to create the experiences you wish to have in your life, you must first understand who you are. You will then apply the normal manifestation techniques to visualize and manifest the outcomes you desire. This is where it gets easier and easier.

Find out about your own integral-self and then you will find out what you're truly capable of. As you discover this, you will discover the challenges that may be occurring for you to guide you rather than hinder your success.

That being said I want you to begin creating the outcomes using the manifestation process outlined below. Once you fully understand the principles and commit to the process, you won't believe how easy it is for you.

1. Know what it is that you want.
2. Allow yourself to receive it.

Sounds pretty simple, right?

I will stay firm in my conviction and challenge the work on manifestation that indicates we can create or manifest without understanding the deep-rooted traits that are buried in our unconscious minds first. It's impossible.

Most people will focus primarily on the visualization aspect of manifestation because it is the easiest. It is important to visualize, whether through words, affirmations or meditations, however allowing yourself to receive is of much more importance and often a far more challenging part of the process. Allowing, in essence, is finding your highest form of energy and your own integral-self. When the two become aligned and in tune with one another, your clarity to create that which you desire will greatly improve.

Throughout the course of this book, and the work and exercises you continue to do, you are now more confident than ever before to create new experiences. Your integrity-based desires are what you will focus on, with complete trust in this process.

My suggestion is that as you begin to consider what you would like to manifest that you start small, rather than going for it all right away. This too will aid you in building confidence in the manifestation process.

Having coffee with a spouse during a troubled relationship is a much simpler visualization than healing your entire relationship and living happily ever after.

Visualizing yourself going on a self-discovery retreat away from your current partner is much different than visualizing a divorce coming to fruition.

Do you see the differences here?

These smaller manifestations will give you insight and experience. Smaller amounts of money, minor job changes or goodness for others can be great ways to practice.

Remember to revisit the chapter in trust and faith, as you want to manifest with a full expectation that what you wish to create will come to fruition. This is not an idea but rather a certainty that you will achieve that which you desire. Remember that there is a divine plan for all of us, and faith in that will assist in what you wish to manifest.

There are a couple of principles in manifestation that I want you to get crystal clear on before you apply the process. Many of the outcomes people desire have a fear base to them because people worry their outcomes will not come to fruition. Ask yourself if what you wish to manifest is fear driven or trust based.

Recognize all of the fears associated with any specific outcomes and understand that this is a thought process you have created, and that fear is usually an illusion. If you need to, write out all the fears that pertain to not achieving a specific outcome and then write out all the reasons why there is really no fear associated with it, whatsoever.

This is why it is so important to understand your energy and work with the Universal Law of Vibration. If you are experiencing challenging emotions such as fear, you are ultimately working in a lower vibrational state. Nobody wants to continue to manifest more emotionally challenging or fear-based experiences.

In order to create the positive outcomes you desire, the integral-self will guide you to what is needed to receive. The process that we discuss in the next chapter will take you through cleansing and clearing your integral-self. We will examine your vibration to further determine what energy you are holding.

The second principle to note is that when working with the Law of Attraction, often people are trying to attract from a place of lack and scarcity rather than one of abundance. You already know that what you hope to create exists before you receive it, yet so many of you are hoping, wishing and even praying that what you desire will come to fruition.

Again, lack and scarcity are lower in vibration and you want to avoid attracting more lack and scarcity.

You'll want to create specific outcomes, as if they already exist in absolute abundance. This is where understanding your outcomes and the feeling associated with them is vital. Visualization will assist you in this, and there are many practices to utilize when it comes to manifesting. The key is to understand that your thoughts dictate your reality. Reach for the highest vibration possible at all times and be sure to be in a positive vibrational state when you engage in any manifestation process.

Focus On The Activity, Not The Results

The underlying principle in any creative process you decide to utilize is that you must focus on the activity and not the results. If you are too attached to your outcome, once again you are going to find yourself in a place of lack and scarcity.

My purpose is to shift your mindset to one of integrity and abundance. Once you have shifted, you will then align your intentions (goals), with your actions (commitments), while detaching from the end result. If you do this properly, the results will come.

One of my favourite manifestation techniques is to write yourself a "Letter From The Future." You write the letter as if a specific time period had elapsed when all that you wished to create had come to fruition.

The key to this letter is getting as detailed as possible on what your goals were for the time period stated, and the specific actions that took place in that time period. Again, you are declaring what you wish to create in full detail, however you then outline your commitments to getting there as if they already happened. I write my own letter from the future each and every year around the holiday season and I've been amazed to see how much of it manifests in my life.

One of my coaching clients who we will call "Marty" had stepped out of his marriage and wished to make positive changes to become more integrity-based and to heal. He committed to my full process of discovery, and discovered his own integral-self. As he continued to make progress, he decided to do a Letter From The Future dated January 1st, 2017. He wrote the letter on January 1st, 2016 as if the year had already come and gone. Here's his example:

January 1st, 2017

Dear Marty,

What a year it's been after so much struggle and turmoil in 2016. You began to understand yourself further with the continued support of your mentor and coach, family and the process of creating more integrity.

You finally feel a deep sense of satisfaction for your purpose in life which is serving your family. You completely eliminated the relationship with the woman you had an affair with and have not spoken to her for over eighteen months. This allowed you to begin to create more trust in yourself, your wife and your children.

Your presence at home gives you a greater sense of pride than you have ever felt before. You are now ensuring that you have one date night per week with your wife and you spend one hour per day every day with your children that is completely uninterrupted from work distractions.

Your discovery process continues to lead you to understanding what integrity means to you. You now realize that the relationship you had with your father as a child was not healthy and a poor point of reference. As you have healed much of this relationship with him and internally, you also now see what a great gift the relationship was and how it's created a good opportunity to grow spiritually.

Your specific action steps to increasing integrity are to focus on your body and spiritual work. You committed to losing ten pounds of body fat and to your own disbelief you actually lost twenty. You did this through a commitment to working out five days per week for sixty minutes. You also decreased your fat intake and increased the amount of protein you ate based on a proven process for fitness and nutrition.

For whatever reason, your Real Estate business has exploded. You notice higher energy inside of yourself each and every day which allows you to wake up earlier and earlier. This appears to have a great correlation with the quality and quantity of clients *you attract. Your business generated over $500,000 in gross commissions versus $300,000 the year prior. You also managed to take more time off and dedicated a trip for your tenth year wedding anniversary with your wife.*

Fortunately for you, your wife has seen the action you have been taking when it comes to working on yourself and the steps you have taken to heal your marriage and family life. You continue to support your wife in her own healing as she has indicated she wants the marriage to work.

You do not know what the future holds but you are excited and grateful to be on this path.

You love yourself more and more each day.

Marty

I was very excited for Marty as he continued to manifest and create the experiences he desired. He made a commitment to understanding his integral-self which allowed him to understand why he had created negative outcomes. It was then that he could begin to create positive outcomes. He manifested everything he wrote down in his own letter from the future, and you can too.

Another path for manifestation is to utilize meditation, which I'm a strong advocate of. Again there are many ways to meditate and the information available is abundant. I recommend this for those that have meditative experience and concentrate well. The basic principles are as follows:

1. Hold a vision of your goal in your mind for two to three minutes until it is crystal clear.
2. Use your imagination to visualize that which you desire to manifest.
3. Enjoy thinking about your creation as if you had manifested it in full detail.

4. Experience the energy and feelings associated with your desire.
5. Bring the experience of the excited feelings associated with your manifestation back to you throughout your day.

A coaching client who I worked with had three children and her marriage was suffering terribly. Her husband had been having inappropriate relationships for years and the quantity of these relationships was higher than any client I've worked with in the past. Despite a deep knowing of her preference to leave the relationship and pursue a new life, my client was fearful of the effect that divorce would have on her children and what others would think of her.

We worked through her own Integrity Vows which led to great confidence in understanding herself and why she continued to choose men that betrayed her. After all, her father was never present at home and had many of his own indiscretions. This was her point of reference that she needed to heal first, and then begin to understand how she could create new and more integrity-based experiences. She was highly intuitive and very committed so we felt that a meditative practice would work well for her.

First she established that the creation she desired primarily applied to her own happiness so that she could give the best of herself to her children. She also wanted to establish a clear strategy to exit her marriage and find compassion for her husband and herself in the experience. Finally, she wanted to discover a way to visualize and create the healthiest experience for her children when it came to her divorce.

I first had her begin with a guided meditation that focused on her root chakra which places an emphasis on grounding. This allowed her to gain confidence and strength for the decision to leave her marriage. It also was a great initial ritual to keep her consistently focusing on herself and positive emotions.

Secondly, we had her go through a visualization process that placed a focus on the heart chakra. This allowed her to open herself to grace and compassion for her husband. It also allowed her to experience forgiveness and healing for others as well as herself. As she began to open her heart to her current experiences, she also began to visualize and associate with the positive feelings of being single. This was a profound experience for her that allowed her to make a clear decision to end her marriage. It also began to resonate with her because as she began to open her heart, she began to heal and see the possibility of exciting new opportunities. Divorce would not be a hindrance, but rather part of her spiritual growth and divine life path.

Finally I coached her on a deep-rooted Tonglen meditation which is one that allows the healing of others and the self. It allowed her to focus on the pain that her children may be experiencing and to visualize the healthiest version of her children possible. In this she was also able to visualize the healthiest version of herself.

Over the course of six months, she and her husband separated amicably and her children experienced a relatively smooth adjustment. She credits most of her experience to understanding her integral-self, and committing to raising her own vibration through the meditative work described above.

Another commitment to manifest more of what you desire is to visualize on a regular basis through a process of declaration. I recommend journaling or public declaration in order to do this best. Public declaration is when you tell other people what your intentions are.

An example would be to create a vision board and focus on it daily for thirty days. Another would be to identify your ideal manifestation and do a gratitude journal in regards to everything your ideal creation or manifestation means to you.

A recent coaching client of mine entered my program and was considering an inappropriate relationship. While he was not married, his girlfriend and he had been high school sweethearts and they had been together for over fifteen years.

He was fearful he had not had enough life experience and felt that some of the recent flirting and interaction with another friend might provide him with more excitement.

We discussed integrity and began the initial process of creating his custom program to determine his highest and most integral-self. While he did not want to focus on the overall outcome of his current relationship, understanding himself further was crucial. It was also important to stay in integrity through the process.

He began a gratitude journal for the relationship that he had with his girlfriend, only we created this in future form. He wrote down three different experiences he hoped to create with her in the next ten years and the feelings associated with each. He did this consistently for thirty days straight and in that time he did not step outside of his relationship.

He was amazed to notice that several of his ideal manifestations began to become a reality, even though he had declared they would happen in one to two years' time. His progress continues and he remains happily committed to his girlfriend.

Creating and manifesting what you desire can apply to any outcome or experience you'd like to come to fruition. In understanding your own Integrity Vows first, you can then determine how to work with the Law of Vibration and the Law of Attraction at a highly effective level.

Let's revisit the Universal Law of Attraction and gain a clearer understanding of the principles.

THE UNIVERSAL LAW OF ATTRACTION

We already discussed the Universal Law of Vibration and Universal Law of Attraction in Chapter Two. I feel it is important that you understand a few extra principles here. Internalize them.

We attract into our lives what we are offering from a vibrational standpoint. This is why working with the Law of Vibration is so important. Understanding higher vibration versus lower vibration is crucial to your success in manifestation.

Understanding your emotions is a critical element in working with the Universal Laws of Vibration and Attraction.

We attract what we are, not what we want. Simply visualizing that which we desire is not the key component to manifestation.

Visualization is, however, an important tool to utilize in this process to create a different emotional response and different feelings pertaining to that which you wish to create.

The emotional response of what you visualize is what will fuel your vibration and point of attraction. This is the way that you power your attraction magnet.

Understanding your integral-self will allow you to work with visualization and allowing. Without an understanding of your emotions, beliefs and previous manifestations, often you will continue to create similar experiences.

Remember, you hold the power to attract whatever you desire.

CHAPTER 13 EXERCISES

The exercises here will assist you in furthering your exploration and dedication on what you wish to create in your life. My hope is that by now you understand the true magnitude of the power you hold when it comes to the manifestation process.

1. What is one outcome you would like to achieve?
2. What is one small step you can take to begin manifesting that outcome?
3. Write your own "Letter From The Future."
4. Write down one challenge you may be experiencing and visualize how you could find resolution. Journal all of your answers in the Integrity Vow Workbook.

A Gateway To Integrity

"The strongest thing that any human being has going is their own integrity and their own heart. As soon as you start veering away from that, the solidity that you need in order to be able to stand up for what you believe in and deliver what's really inside, it's just not going to be there."

-Herbie Hancock

Have you made a decision?

Is it time to express the highest and most integral-version of you?

Are you ready to commit to change?

Ultimately, that is what this book is about. It is an ongoing discovery of your own path to your most integral-self, and a transformative process to continually access it.

Although the process may seem daunting at times, the choices are simple if you decide to take action. I have seen various levels of transformation both in my own life and with the clients I have worked with. My clients have all experienced many degrees of transformation. I am certain that, while outcomes may vary for each individual, this process works.

I do not have all of the answers on how the Universe will guide you, however I am confident that manifesting new experiences and creating your integral-self is completely possible.

When you understand, imagine and create your soul's true vision, you will find just how real it gets. You will begin to examine your goals and commitment level, and to align your intentions with your actions. Your results will come to fruition like never before and your integral-self will thank you.

Whatever your background and however you wish to describe it, whether it's God, Source, Buddha or the Universe, the possibilities are endless when it comes to creating that which you desire.

The power is within you, and only you, to make this decision. Once you allow yourself to work with the powerful Universal Laws versus working against them, your manifestation ability will develop.

When my wife read this book she said that she was upset because she felt like the man she originally married was not who she thought he was. She was totally correct in this as I had not discovered much of my integral-self at the time we got engaged.

She indicated that she didn't realize I'd had so many challenges or had not explored the various parts of myself that would not serve our marriage well. This was true.

There was resentment and frustration because I had not been transparent about who I was when we got engaged. I didn't realize that I should have self-discovered and understood my own integrity before making such a serious commitment.

What I shared with her was that I didn't realize those parts of myself existed when I asked her to marry me. Everything shows up to serve us as an opportunity to evolve spiritually, however understanding and utilizing a process like this could have saved most of the pain involved in my marriage.

Integrity is something that we can continually access more of. I am forever grateful that my wife's integrity and empathy granted me the compassion to continue doing the work that I do, heal myself and be a better father. I'm even more grateful that as I stepped into my own integrity and realized our marriage was going to end, we were both fortunate to heal and remain friends. She's the most courageous human being I've ever met and I'm honoured to have her as the mother of my children.

It was also crucial that she understood it wasn't something that she did or didn't do that created the end of our marriage. It wasn't that she wasn't good enough or didn't give her very best effort. It was more about my own clarity and realization that I was not in integrity if I remained in our relationship.

Whether it's a relationship or your physical health or profession you'd like to change, there is not one specific definition for your success. Every single one of us has different circumstances that make up our current experience. One thing I am certain of when it comes to finding success in this process, however, is:

Transparency will yield you better results.

The choice to understand your integral-self is up to you. It's your decision to discover and unravel both the darkness and light that exist deep within your core being. The journey to your integral-self is an ongoing and a lifelong process of creation. It is one which I hope you embrace at the most transparent and authentic level.

Once you make the decision to change and apply this process with a transparent approach, you will receive divine universal guidance. You will utilize the tools you have learned in this book, your intuition and of course the Universe itself.

Often you will notice that by staying true to your integral-self, and with a highly committed approach to your creations, you will begin to see transformation and manifestation occurring in a few weeks or even days.

I realize this may be hard to believe, but client after client of mine continues to experience dramatic results in short periods of time.

Someone once asked me to summarize the coaching process and accountability platform that I facilitate. They wanted step-by-step details on how to utilize the principles involved for transformation purposes. For our purpose in this book, I will share as many tips and techniques as possible, although my one-one-one coaching program is tailored differently to every client. It is difficult to summarize as the Integrity Vow process unfolds differently for everyone.

I have certain clients begin my program with a complete knowing of what they wish to change beyond just their businesses. I have others who have committed to only business growth, but after six or eight weeks often admit they are having addiction challenges or relationship issues. Everyone is at a different stage of their journey.

Although the commitment to one's integral-self is the purpose of my coaching, I summarize it as a true place of discovery. What would bring forth the highest and most integral version of you? What changes need to occur in order for that to happen? What specific steps will you make to create your own Integrity Vows?

As the title of this chapter indicates, the process I offer you, including the work you've completed in this book, is a gateway to understanding yourself further and defining your own integral-path. In essence, they are stepping stones to create your vision and utilize the necessary steps to finding the happiness and freedom you desire.

It is then up to you to commit to the work on an ongoing and consistent basis. This is not a one-stop shop for self-worth or self-help. This is a lifetime commitment, and often one of many lifetimes, in order to continually understand yourself and achieve the highest state of consciousness possible.

Now is the time to get very transparent about what you wish to create in your own experience. This is where you begin to determine your own path to your integral-self. As we begin the process I will ask that you take a full inventory of your current experiences to determine what parts of the process need to be addressed first. Here are some different aspects to consider as you begin:

If you have done any form of coaching before, have you been held accountable by your mentor or coach? What kind of results did you achieve in previous coaching or mentoring including any work that you've done that was self-administered? An example of self-administered work would be personal development work such as reading this book.

Based on the results that you achieved in the past, what would you consider were success factors, and what appeared to challenge your success? Journal your responses in the Integrity Vow Workbook.

Some other self-reflection to consider is to determine what may potentially be preventing you from moving into your most integral-self like never before.

Consider what gets in the way of commitment. Remember that goals are nice in theory, however unless you align your intentions with your integrity and then take action, the results will often be minimal. What consistently gets in the way, whether in your past or present experience, of you taking committed action steps on a regular basis? Journal your responses now.

What aspects of your current experience do you feel require the most change and growth? What areas of your personal Integrity Vow do you need to discover in order to set goals and achieve them? Where are you experiencing the most struggles in your life? This could include personal, professional, physical or health challenges. Journal your findings now.

Perhaps your relationship is suffering and you want to discover why and create healthier outcomes inside of it. You may also have experienced or been involved with infidelity and need to decide whether to stay in or leave a relationship. You may also be on the verge of making an unhealthy decision to step outside of your relationship. Whatever it is for you, this process will assist and guide you.

Are you feeling trapped inside of a relationship with a circumstance, addiction or other human being? Are you experiencing a spiritual fracture because your actions are not aligned with your integral-self?

Are you on the verge of creating chaos in your life and do you want to create something different for yourself before it's too late? Do you want to ensure you make a healthy choice so that you do not negatively impact the lives of others? Are you tired of continuing to create patterns that you've been creating all along?

Have you been betrayed by anyone, whether it's a family member, friend or colleague, and do you want to cultivate more self-worth to either reconcile the relationship or rid yourself of an association once and for all? Discovering your integrity through this process will assist in creating clarity for big decisions.

Whatever you are experiencing in current space and time and whatever it is that you desire to change, the power is within you and it's in the present moment, meaning NOW. This is your opportunity to take a stand for yourself and grow spiritually to create your highest form of integrity.

Before you commit further to the work I've outlined in this book or will review with you in the overall Integrity Vow process, you must make the choice to change. I believe that you already have, in that you've read this far, but stay in that place of increased awareness in order to commit further. Sometimes declaring this to friends and family is a positive exercise in affirming your commitment. Remember that public declaration has a profound impact on manifestation.

I understand that it can be painful, scary and challenging to make this decision. You will experience a series of different emotions and outcomes as you move through the process. You will have moments when you want to quit and give up. You will find success in certain areas and feel confident that you are doing all the right things and then face more challenges at times.

Sometimes you may feel like a failure, but remember that every outcome we create is an opportunity to learn, grow and evolve as spiritual beings.

I've had many of my clients commit to this process and experience amazing success only to fall off track at times. We are all human, myself included. My commitment to fitness and nutrition can be hindered like anyone's but the difference is that anytime I fall off track, out of my own integrity, or lose the momentum I created, I know that I have the power to make the choice to recommit. And I do.

I'm not suggesting that you go into this with a mediocre approach to it either. It doesn't work that way. What I want you to do is hold some compassion for yourself along the way. What you are striving to create is a new normal and a new commitment to your most integral-self. All of your experiences will then unfold more naturally, creating the outcomes you desire and deserve.

I also want you to use caution when understanding the negative choices and painful parts of your past. I caution you about coaching with any mentor that focuses only on the dark and negative parts of your experience. Understand what those parts of you are, however constantly grant compassion, forgiveness and grace to others and yourself. Always work towards a higher vibration.

90-DAY INTEGRITY VOW PROCESS

This is a great time to visit www.TheIntegrityVow.com/Resources and print out my 90-Day Integrity Calendar.

This 90-Day Integrity Vow process will aid you from beginning to end if you revisit every chapter in this book and examine how each one may apply to you. Studying the Universal Laws associated with each chapter and revisiting the exercises will support you even further.

Because everyone is different, and everyone creates or manifests differently, I will re-examine some of the principles with you in order to support your individual experience. This is the same process that most of my one-on-one coaching clients enter, and the direction I take with each client depends on what each one wishes to change and what outcome each one is interested in creating. Again, this process is an outline. Most of my one-on-one coaching clients commit to a specific call-time with me each week and the process can move in whatever direction it may. The purpose of this process is to give you some personal guidance and revisit the principles learned in this book.

The process is also determined by each individual's commitment level and how well he or she responds to accountability. Everyone experiences this differently, and how transparent and forthright a person is in our initial process will also determine the individual's specific program. Remember that this is a model I work from as each individual's journey unfolds differently.

If you are fully prepared to be transparent and authentic regarding your current experience and how you desire change, I welcome you to begin the Integrity Vow process now.

WEEK 1 (DAYS 1 TO 7): DISCOVERING YOUR INTEGRITY

The first part of this process is to have you determine what your own Integrity Vow is and get a very clear vision of what it means to you. You may not have the answers right away, which is totally fine. It's a continual process of self-discovery and self-reflection. Exploring your own values and what integrity means to you is a life-long journey, and they may change over time.

In Chapter One I outlined the general principles of integrity and why Universal Laws are important in working with your own Integrity Vow.

The key to your success revolves around three critical areas I want you to consider right here and now.

1. Transparency: What is happening in your current experience, both personally and professionally, that you desire change in?
2. Choice: Are you declaring that you are making a choice to create positive changes in your life right here and right now?
3. Commitment: You can visualize all that you want, but unless you commit to specific and executable action steps, the vision is just an idea.

The process begins with a commitment by you to bring forth transparency, integrity and the choice to change via commitment to a proven accountability process.

Although I will have you write a Letter From The Future, as discussed in Chapter Thirteen, very early on in our process, we begin with a Letter From The Future for a 90-Day Period.

The first ninety days will be the most challenging and can also yield you the greatest results. Write a letter to yourself dated ninety days from now on everything that you created and manifested in that time period. Revisit Chapter Thirteen for more specific instruction on Letters From The Future.

Week 2 (Days 8 to 14):

In Chapter Two, we placed an emphasis on the Universal Law of Vibration and the Universal Law of Attraction. You've already outlined what you are going to manifest in your Letter From The Future and now it's time to begin doing just that.

Pay special attention to the Universal Law of Cause and Effect, which we discussed in Chapter Two. Take an inventory of some of the recent choices you have made and what consequences are unfolding, whether they are positive or negative. Your current experience may be affecting your vibration, and ensuring you are aware of this is absolutely crucial.

In order to create more positive outcomes you'll need to increase your vibration to the highest level possible. It is important to ensure that you are in an optimal receiving state for your manifestations to come to fruition. This is where we refer to your point of attraction.

The three areas of focus to improve your own vibration and point of attraction are Body, Mind and Spirit.

BODY

When I first began working out and committing to a proper nutrition plan, I did not realize there would be a direct correlation between the work that I did to nurture my body and every other experience in my life. The same holds true for nearly all of my coaching clients and others who have studied my work.

Unlike many transformation processes, I'm not requesting that you decide to become a professional athlete, bodybuilder or fitness model. Your dedication to your body must feel right for you, and allowing yourself to discover this feeling will then support your overall commitment level.

What I encourage in your own place of discovery comes from accepted research and numerous studies. Placing an emphasis on health and fitness is documented and proven to have a positive impact on your relationships and your self-worth.

Remember that much of this book allowed you to discover areas where low self-worth were created, which in turn affects your vibration and what you tend to attract. My purpose is to assist you in discovering a higher vibration, more self-worth and a much stronger and more positive point of attraction.

Every single one of my coaching clients has discovered improvements when he or she implemented and committed to fitness and health. Many have also indicated they notice a direct correlation to improving their relationships, finding financial abundance and achieving their highest and most integral-self. This was the same result I experienced when working with some of my own guides and mentors.

Finding your healthiest state to manifest is important and a key determining factor for progress. A commitment to health, and eliminating any substance abuse or addictions will only serve you well in this area.

Pause here and consider where you are on a scale of one to ten as it applies to your self-image, body weight or the way that your clothes fit. Again, I'm not asking for you to be the next Mr. or Mrs.

Universe (no pun intended), however I want you to ask yourself if you desire growth and change in this area.

It's always amazing to me that most people want the physical change more than anything. They also realize that this commitment will lead to healthier and more integral versions of themselves, however they fail to truly commit in this space. In my experience, this is a direct reflection of the experiences from early childhood that instilled aspects of low self-worth in each individual. Uncovering these experiences and healing from them will assist in the physical transformation.

I believe that you will see exceptional results if you commit to working on your physical fitness and health over the next ninety days.

While an ideal workout program includes four to five workouts per week for sixty to ninety minutes each, we will create a suitable program for each client's comfort level and capacity. The custom programs I provide are different for each client I work with. To serve you in this process, I will provide sample workouts or learning aids that you can find at www.TheIntegrityVow.com/resources. You will also continue to examine your diet and make changes with regards to your protein and carbohydrate intake, along with eliminating unnecessary fats and extras that don't serve your highest nutritional needs.

If you are currently an alcohol drinker and are comfortable committing to the ninety day process without alcohol, I guarantee you will see a dramatic difference in many areas of your life. This is a commitment only you can make for yourself.

One of the other major elements of working out is that it is one of the ideal states to create or manifest in. When you work out your body releases chemicals that make you feel good, and feeling good means that your vibration rises. There is an excellent opportunity to work on some of your creative and manifestation techniques while working out.

I also recommend that you eliminate watching television or listening to anything that is not positive while you work out. Sad old love songs are not going to serve you well in any relationship status, and it's important to recognize what you're putting between your ears and allowing your mind to absorb. Consider if what you're normally listening to is angry, crude or sad.

My favourite types of listening for the purposes of manifestation during a workout are personal development audio books or higher vibrational music. Higher vibrational music such as dance, trance, house or techno often increase your beats per minute and can serve you very well when it comes to using your imagination during a workout. Working out in complete silence is also another positive option. Test and try what works best for you.

MIND

Although many of my clients enter my coaching for the purpose of business, very clearly we examine and investigate the mind from a place of clarity and presence. Your spiritual work will assist you in this if you apply it on a daily basis, but for the purpose of this section and your ninety days, let's look at some of the aspects in this book that we will apply in our process.

Chapters Three, Four, Five and Six discussed certain topics that may be brought forth in your current experience. Perhaps you are challenged in a relationship where trust and violation is an issue. We will examine self-worth, attachment, addiction and any unhealthy outcomes that you are currently creating. We will discuss and determine the correlation between these discoveries and the experiences you are currently creating.

Although this book places a strong emphasis on your integrity and how it pertains to your personal relationships, these thirty days provide a place of discovery for all of your experiences.

If you have been betrayed or are considering stepping out of your own integrity, much of the work on control in Chapter Four will resonate here. This is a good time to check in and consider what aspects of addiction or attachment you may be experiencing as well. The more you uncover and understand the causes of these attachments and addictions, the more self-worth you will create. This too will aid in your manifestation process.

Imagine that. You are going to continually work on your own integral-self in order to create better outcomes with others. By shifting your inside world through this process, you will have clarity in making better decisions about your outside world and the relationships you wish to cultivate. You may also determine that certain relationships are unhealthy and no longer serve your integral-self.

In this ninety day process it is crucial to understand that the more you clear your mind and the higher you raise your vibration, the more that you will attract the integrity-based experiences you desire.

If you do have any addictions or attachments that are not allowing you to experience clarity and peace of mind, it is time to make a concrete decision and choice to change. Without doing so your results will be minimal.

If needed, now is the time to be transparent and seek help or guidance for these challenges. If you feel that you're in a situation that presents immediate harm to yourself or someone else, seek immediate attention.

SPIRITUAL GROWTH

While Chapter Three discussed trust and violation, it also emphasised understanding the Universal Law of Resistance in order to further allow your integral-self to come forth.

Much of the ninety day process will require you to self-discover further and evolve spiritually. Some of the information that you learn along the way may seem foreign to you, and that's okay. Spiritual growth is different for everyone and an initial understanding of the principles will support you no matter what.

I want to share that this is an ongoing process of evolution. There is unlimited information available to you in regards to spiritual growth. I will provide you with specific tools and resources, along with a series of rituals to implement. My one-on-one program determines this depending on each client, and I will continue to add resources for you the reader on www.TheIntegrityVow.com.

These tools and rituals will include specific bodies of spiritual work, meditation practices, healing rituals, prayers and various affirmations. Depending on each client's Integrity Vow, they will be different for everyone.

WEEKS 3-6 (DAYS 15 TO 42)

Over the course of this four-week session, an ongoing process of understanding your commitments and what may be getting in the way of your success is crucial.

Each and every day you will look to improve your own vibration and point of attraction, allowing yourself to feel better about your own integral-path. This requires an ongoing commitment to self-awareness.

This month-long commitment often gives a deeper understanding for my coaching clients of where they are making progress or continuing to face challenges.

When my clients remain true to their own Integrity Vows, they begin to discover more and more of the different experiences both in their inside world and their outside world. This is a place of awareness, which allows more to unfold in the process.

As discussed in Chapters Five and Six, allow yourself to discover more about the choices you are making and determine whether you are facing any challenges with addiction. We discussed the differences between addiction and attachment, and this can be a truly transformational point of discovery.

For clients suffering from painful circumstances such as addiction, obsession and even betrayal, often utilizing the Universal Law of Detachment discussed in Chapter Six will have an impact. This is challenging to say the least. Often times my clients and I spend ample time in this space to experience attachment and invoke detachment.

Whether you are in my one-on-one program or determining your Integrity Vow here, you will need to align your intentions and actions. Depending on each individual experience, pausing here to truly understand the Universal Law of Intention and The Universal Law of Action may be crucial.

The entire month is dedicated to self-discovery and paying close attention to the body, mind and spirit. The commitment to health, nutrition, energy, vibration and what my clients begin to attract is consistent at all times. The process and various commitments each client makes along with the recommended accountability steps are often unique to the individual.

Due to this part of the process being over an extended period of time, I highly encourage you to journal every day. Get your thoughts out of your mind and in writing. This will bring forth much clarity, as journaling can be a profound exercise in healing and manifestation.

WEEKS 7 AND 8 (DAYS 43 TO 56)

Chapters Seven and Eight investigate Truth and Transparency along with Grace and Gratitude. The Universal Laws that we apply in my process here are Relativity and Allowing.

Remember that defining your Integrity Vow or visualizing that which you wish to create is only one step of the process. Allowing yourself to receive and get into the state of receiving is far more crucial to the art of manifestation.

Often times when clients enter my program, they are experiencing high levels of pain. Whether it's addiction, obsession, attachment or low self-worth, they may also be experiencing denial. Often their relationships are in jeopardy or have already been jeopardized.

The process of determining your own integral-self also requires you to understand your past and how it is impacting your current experience. This too can be very painful both emotionally and physically, to examine past experiences and how they affect your current reality.

Although every client differs, and some may experience discomfort halfway through the ninety days, I find that those that commit to increasing their vibration and detaching from negativity are often willing to commit further. It's sometimes challenging to create new standards for yourself, but it will be very worthwhile.

In many cases, this is a point where clients move away from denial or resistance and towards allowing and/or acceptance. They are often encouraged by their own self-discovery and examining the past. Chapter Seven discussed the truth about the self and bringing the most transparent aspects of the self forward into every circumstance.

Again, this is not always easy, but by granting grace to others and yourself, along with finding gratitude for all of your experiences, you move into a greater state of receiving as discussed in Chapter Eight.

Week 9 (Days 57 to 63)

I have paid a great amount of attention in this book to the associations that we keep and the relationships we have. This includes relationships with others and that with the self. I have referenced many of my own personal experiences and those of specific coaching clients.

In Chapter Nine we investigated the Law of Association and utilizing it for your own self-discovery. In this week a full inventory of the relationships that you have with others and yourself is examined.

Often this is a challenging week for those that are focusing on their relationship status with a partner. Often times it can be a very revealing week to determine if certain associations need to cease and what boundaries with others must be created.

In order to experience the highest and most integral-self, often the boundaries we create don't simply exist with others. More often than not, they have to do with the relationship we have with ourselves. A full investigation of our own associations and the possibility of creating new associations and boundaries is explored in this week and on an ongoing basis.

Week 10 (Days 64 to 70)

While the path of awareness and a commitment to your integral-self is the process, often we have ongoing temptations in various circumstances.

My purpose is to continue to create tools, strategies and an ongoing accountability program to serve you during and well after the ninety day commitment and reading of this book.

In Chapter Ten we examined Temptation and Honour and what that truly means to you. Understanding temptation and working with the Universal Law of Dharma will allow you to remain committed.

In this week we'll also examine purpose and how honouring your own can bring you fulfillment, creativity and further direction. Remember to reflect and journal in your Integrity Vow Workbook on what purpose means to you. Remember that everyone has a purpose in life and it's a wonderful discovery for you to make.

Week 11 (Days 71 to 77)

As you head towards the last several weeks of these ninety days, it's important to self-reflect and self-appreciate. Often times we can all get sidetracked or lose momentum. At other times we may not get the results that we desire right away.

This week, you will focus on the Universal Law of Pure Potential as discussed in Chapter Eleven. Your possibilities are endless when you have faith in the process and yourself.

My hope is that you also begin to recognize that there is more than just our internal experience that is occurring. The Universe has a divine plan for all of us when it comes to that which we wish to manifest, whether it's financial abundance, finding love or creating new relationships.

WEEKS 12 AND 13 (DAYS 78 TO 90)

Whatever it is that your integral-self desires, often it takes courage to make serious and profound choices to grow. It takes courage to understand your current circumstances and make choices in order to embrace true spiritual evolution.

In the last two weeks of the ninety-day process we discover areas where you may need to be more courageous in order to manifest and create your ideal experiences and outcomes. We revisit the Universal Law of Acceptance and the Universal Law of Love. Journeying further towards your integral-self, the love of self and love of others is of utmost importance. It is important that you continue your commitments to journaling and rituals that I've outlined for you in all of the exercises.

Finally, we address your creative and manifestation processes as addressed in Chapter Thirteen. We revisit the Universal Law of Attraction and reflect upon the full ninety days and your efforts. Reflection and awareness are crucial as you may want to commit to certain areas or even make changes as you transform through this process.

This is where we will revisit your initial Letter From The Future, manifestation processes and rituals, and overall results to date.

This is a great point to acknowledge yourself for the work that you have done and will continue to do. It is also a perfect opportunity to discover where further work is needed and how you can stay committed to this process for the long term.

SUMMARY

Finding the courage to begin the work in this book is something I must acknowledge you for. Please take a moment to self-appreciate and acknowledge yourself as well.

Whether you've stepped out of integrity or are discovering areas of your life that need change, you've made a commitment to complete this book. Commend yourself on your efforts and remember that what we celebrate tends to expand.

All of the keys to your own evolution are contained in the previous pages, but it may take time and continued effort to allow each key to open each door. My hope is that you will continue to revisit this book and the chapters or areas that apply to you. Come back to it time and time again as I do, and have faith that the Universe is working in your favour.

If you need further assistance or guidance beyond this book, know that I am here to support you. You can find more information about my coaching and consulting organization and visit me online at www.TheIntegrityVow.com

The Universe isn't always fair, however it is perfect.

If you want more, then become more.

May love and light grace your path.

AFTERWORD

I WAS ON A PLANE flying home from a speaking engagement in the United States and I felt an amazing sense of well-being. I was excited to launch my new book, *The Integrity Vow: Engaging Your Authentic Self.* I felt great clarity surrounding the book and was confident that it would impact many people who may be experiencing life in the way that I used to experience it. As the plane glided over the clouds, I felt a calm place of peace inside myself. Although the outer landscape I was viewing through the plane window was serene, it paled in comparison to my internal world which was full of pure bliss and gratitude.

In essence, my life is full of joy, happiness and the freedom I had always desired and knew existed. It was in these moments that I gained more and more reverence for life. As I reflected, I found myself appreciating life the way that I should and I was excited about my next destination, which was home. I would see my amazing children who I love and am constantly amazed by. Nothing brings me more joy than watching my children as their souls expand in their human experience. I am pleased to say that Lisa and I remain good friends, and that we continue to support our children at the highest level. My separation ensured I step further into my integral-self and become a much better father. This was one of the greatest gifts of my life.

I continue to seek guidance on the questions that support my integral-self. I make commitments, practice self-awareness and reflection, and remind myself to recommit at times. The process I mentor others on is one that I must stay aware of to maintaining my own integral-self.

I feel healthy and whole.

BELOW ARE SHORT DESCRIPTIONS FOR each of the Universal Laws that are found in the chapters of this book. I encourage you to explore and embrace all of the Universal Laws that go well beyond these pages.

The Law of Acceptance: There is a greater power than just us as individuals.

The Law of Action: In order to create that which you desire, some form of action must be taken.

The Law of Allowing: We must allow things to evolve naturally and without resistance.

The Law of Association: We become the average of the five people we surround ourselves with the most.

The Law of Attraction: Everything that you are attracting into your life is a direct match to the vibration you are offering.

The Law of Cause and Effect: Every action has a consequence, whether positive or negative.

The Law of Detachment: The law that allows us to release what we feel that it is we desire.

The Law of Dharma: Everything in its entirety has a purpose on this planet.

The Law of Intention: We must direct energy intentionally as the first step in the manifestation process.

The Law of Love: Love is universal energy in its purest form or state.

The Law of Pure Potential: There are no limits to what any of us can do in the life that we have been given.

The Law of Relativity: Everyone and everything has challenges and tests that we experience, and these experiences all allow us to learn and grow spiritually.

The Law of Resistance: Anything that is offering resistance will create or manifest more of the same.

The Law of Vibration: Everything in the Universe has a vibration.

33699926R00140